THE ST. MARTIN'S
SOURCEBOOK
FOR WRITING TUTORS

THE ST. MARTIN'S SOURCEBOOK FOR WRITING TUTORS

Christina Murphy
TEXAS CHRISTIAN UNIVERSITY

Steve Sherwood
TEXAS CHRISTIAN UNIVERSITY

ST. MARTIN'S PRESS

NEW YORK

Senior editor: Marilyn Moller
Development : Susan Cottenden
Managing editor: Patricia Mansfield Phelan
Project editor: Amy Horowitz
Cover design: Sheree Goodman

Manufactured in the United States of America.   \

9 8 7
f e

For information, write:
St. Martin's Press, Inc.
175 Fifth Avenue
New York, NY 10010

ISBN: 0-312-11729-9

Acknowledgments
Jeff Brooks. "Minimalist Tutoring: Making the Student Do All the Work." *Writing Lab Newsletter* 15.6 (1991): 1–4.
Irene Lurkis Clark. "Collaboration and Ethics in Writing Center Pedagogy." *Writing Center Journal* 9.1 (1988): 3–12.
Anne DiPardo. "'Whispers of Coming and Going' : Lessons from Fannie." *Writing Center Journal* 12.2 (1992): 125–44.
Toby Fulwiler. "Provocative Revision," *Writing Center Journal* 12.2 (1992): 190–204.
Cynthia Haynes-Burton. "'Thirty-something' Students: Concerning Transitions in the Writing Center." *Writing Lab Newsletter* 18.8 (1994): 3–4.
Shoshana Beth Konstant. "Multi-sensory Tutoring for Multi-sensory Learners." *Writing Lab Newsletter* 16.9–10 (1992): 6–8.
Andrea Lunsford. "Collaboration, Control, and the Idea of a Writing Center." *Writing Center Journal* 12.1 (1991): 3–10.
Christina Murphy. "Freud in the Writing Center: The Psychoanalytics of Tutoring Well." *Writing Center Journal* 10.1 (1989): 13–18.
Stephen North. "The Idea of a Writing Center." *College English* September 1984. Copyright 1984 by the National Council of Teachers of English. Reprinted with permission.
Judith K. Powers. "Rethinking Writing Center Conferencing Strategies for the ESL Writer." *Writing Center Journal* 13.2 (1993): 39–47.
Steve Sherwood. "Humor and the Serious Tutor." *Writing Center Journal.* 13.2 (1993): 3–12.

PREFACE

In planning *The St. Martin's Sourcebook for Writing Tutors*, we began with the question of what knowledge would be most valuable to writing tutors in assisting the learning processes of others. We concluded that tutors would benefit from having an overview of the tutoring process, a sense of the philosophical issues that influence writing center practice, and information on resources for further inquiry. These three concerns are reflected in this book, particularly in the scholarly essays we have chosen to include. These essays focus on both technique and theory, portraying tutoring as a process of interpersonal and social negotiation—one that merits investigation, interpretation, and debate.

We hope that this book will fill a niche between manuals that teach beginners simple tutoring techniques and philosophical treatises that too often divorce theory from practice. We envision this book as a personal guide and resource for tutors that will allow them to see tutoring as an ongoing, evolving process that they will help define.

Of the many people we wish to thank, Marilyn Moller and Susan Cottenden, our editors at St. Martin's, were especially helpful in providing insight, guidance, and exceptional advice in developing this manuscript. We also wish to thank our reviewers, Tim Barnet, Chris DaVinne (both of Ohio State University); Christine Cozzens (Agnes Scott College); and Maura Taffe (Wright State University) whose insightful comments helped guide our revisions. Their assistance and support reflected the best ideals and collaborative spirit of writing center practice.

Finally, we express our appreciation to Mary Sherwood, Frida Blumenberg, Joe Law, Mary Lane, Margaret-Rose Marek, and Mary Nell Kivikko for the patience, kindness, and encouragement that good friends provide.

Christina Murphy
Steve Sherwood

CONTENTS

THE ST. MARTIN'S
SOURCEBOOK
FOR WRITING TUTORS

PART

1

The Tutoring Process: Exploring Paradigms and Practices

We begin *The St. Martin's Sourcebook for Writing Tutors* with the principal ideas that will guide our discussion of the tutoring process and the tutor's role in writing instruction:

- *Tutoring is contextual.* Tutoring takes place within a number of sociocultural and interpersonal contexts that lend richness and complexity to the tutor's role. An understanding of these contexts extends the tutor's technical skill.
- *Tutoring is collaborative.* Tutoring is grounded in interpersonal transactions; it is, fundamentally, a *relationship* more than a body of techniques or even a body of knowledge. In the tutoring session, two people work together toward a common goal; they collaborate. The purpose of the collaboration is to assist writers in their own development. The dialogue between tutor and student—a conversation with a definite purpose—is the basis upon which tutors and students build a supportive, working relationship. Thus, tutoring offers a conceptual and interpersonal framework for the sharing of ideas.
- *Tutoring is interpersonal.* Tutors must draw upon extensive interpersonal skills to work effectively with students who bring a range of educational and cultural backgrounds and a variety of learning styles to their tutoring sessions. As tutors, we need effective interpersonal skills because our purpose is to meet the needs of individual writers.
- *Tutoring is individualized.* If there is any one truth about tutoring, it is that no single method of tutoring, no one approach, will work effectively with every student in every situation. Each tutor develops a style of tutoring primarily from experience, and experience is always a dynamic process of change. Tutoring sessions are as unique and individual as the students who come to be tutored.

With tutoring's complex philosophical background and its rich interpersonal dynamic, you might wonder, "Can I be an effective tutor?" The answer is "yes"—because you are already engaged in the essence of tutoring, which is conversation. With your teachers and fellow students, you have had numerous discussions of the writing process and of how writers learn to improve their work. Now, as a writing center tutor, you will build on these discussions with new thoughts and ideas from conversations with your fellow peer tutors and your writing center mentors. You will also have this sourcebook to enhance your understanding of the tutoring process.

The St. Martin's Sourcebook for Writing Tutors is not a philosophical treatise that separates theory from practice. Nor is it a how-to book of procedures and tactics. Such a simple technique-driven approach would be inadequate for operating in the fluid, unpredictable, give-and-take atmosphere of the tutorial. While tutoring is generally logical, it is seldom tactical; that is, it is not possible to learn a single method and apply it in all instances. Such a scenario fails to describe the complexity and richness of the encounters between tutor and writer.

Rather than a single scenario, then, we have chosen to present multiple views of tutorials and multiple commentaries upon the learning experiences those tutorials embody. The essays here represent a valuable body of knowledge for both the novice and the experienced tutor. In them, we hear many voices commenting on the practice of tutoring—the hows, whys, why nots, shoulds, and should nots—together with the lines of reasoning and the personal experiences that support these viewpoints. We hear of success and failure and starting over again, of the continual rediscovery tutoring represents as both a learning and a teaching experience. We hear the voices of theorists who are accomplished professionals in the field as well as the voices of beginning tutors who are new to the field. We hear the voices of students who have come to tutors seeking knowledge, assistance, and reassurance. Above all, we hear the essence of tutoring: *conversation*. And we begin to realize that there is a broad, interdisciplinary, and theoretical conversation surrounding the practice of tutoring—a conversation this sourcebook invites you to join.

TUTORING AND THE PARADIGMS
OF WRITING INSTRUCTION

As a method for teaching writing, tutoring has been influenced by the *paradigms* that have shaped writing instruction during the past several decades. Tutoring has also been instrumental in shaping those paradigms, largely because writing center tutorials provide practical opportunities to test theoretical assumptions about how students develop as writers.

Since writing centers first appeared on the U.S. educational scene in the 1930s, three paradigms have predominated as models of how writing should be taught: current traditional rhetoric, expressivism (also sometimes called expressionism), and social constructionism.

Current traditional rhetoric focuses almost exclusively on the writer's text and its formal dimensions of grammatical correctness. A writing center tutor who adopts this approach would be concerned with isolating errors and formal weaknesses in a student's text and providing information on how those problems could be corrected.

Because writing centers emerged at a time when current traditional rhetoric was the dominant paradigm, they often tended to take on the role of providing this kind of remedial help to students. As a consequence, writing centers became known, early on, as grammar "fix-it shops," as Stephen M. North puts it in "The Idea of a Writing Center" (on p. 22). In his essay, North opposes limiting writing center instruction to issues of grammatical correctness. Instead, he favors giving more attention to the writer than to the text—especially to how the writer can learn to become more fluent in expressing ideas. In his essay, he describes a model for such a perspective, one that is based on the philosophy of expressivism.

Expressivism, represented by the works of Peter Elbow, Donald Murray, and Ken Macrorie, dominated writing instruction from the 1970s to the mid-1980s. In this paradigm, writing is viewed as a means of self-discovery. By exploring language as a mode of self-expression, students come to know themselves and to develop an "authentic voice" in their writing. Expressivists tend to value the individual writer as a solitary creator who communicates ideas through personal explorations of language, experience, and individual identity.

An expressivist tutor explores the student's understanding of the writing process, particularly the stages of invention and drafting, in which the writer generates ideas and seeks an authentic voice. Expressivist tutors often employ "the Socratic dialogue," asking *heuristic*, or exploratory, questions as a way of getting the student to discover and think about ideas and how they can best be communicated.

North's essay and Jeff Brooks's "Minimalist Tutoring: Making the Student Do All the Work" (on p. 83) discuss in detail the philosophy of expressivist tutoring and the tutor's role within a Socratic dialogue. But as you will discover in Andrea Lunsford's "Collaboration, Control, and the Idea of a Writing Center" (on p. 36), not all theorists view expressivism as a genuinely liberating form of writing instruction. Lunsford, for example, argues that the Socratic dialogue of the expressivist tutor can *seem* to be a freely structured exploration of ideas when, in fact, the tutor's so-called heuristic questions are actually *leading* questions—ones that lead the student toward conclusions already known and valued by the tutor. Lunsford also contends that expressivism places too much emphasis on the individual writer while minimizing or ignoring the social dimensions of language, knowledge, and writing. As a consequence, she argues against the limited scope of expressivism in favor of the philosophy of social constructionism.

While current traditional rhetoric emphasizes the writer's text and expressivism emphasizes the writer's creative processes, *social constructionism* focuses on the sociocultural and historical settings in which writers develop their understanding of language and knowledge. Social constructionism began to affect writing instruction in the mid-1980s and has become one of the dominant paradigms for writing instruction. The most noted advocates of social constructionism are Kenneth A. Bruffee, Marilyn M. Cooper, and Patricia Bizzell. As Lunsford's essay indicates, social constructionists do not believe in the romantic image of the writer as a solitary genius who only has to look inward to find the truth of self-expression. They maintain that knowledge, rather than being "found" uniquely through self-discovery, is "made" by agreement, or consensus, within discourse communities. For example, we as tutors come to have similar ways of talking (and thinking) about our work; other groups form other discourse communities.

The writing center practice advocated by social constructionists involves extensive use of peer group critiquing to reflect the workings of discourse communities and to downplay the role of the tutor as an authority figure or the single source of knowledge. Thus, collaboration and collaborative learning play a more important role in social constructionist writing instruction. The tutor's voice is only one of many the writer will hear, and the tutor and writer are co-learners who collaborate to negotiate meanings and construct knowledge.

As a tutor, you will discover that tutorials are rarely, if ever, exclusively the product of any one paradigm. Instead, they are often a creative, and highly individual, mix of each approach, as the needs of the student dictate. This philosophical complexity adds richness and challenge to the tutor's role and provides ongoing learning experiences in which to refine and personalize a tutoring style.

THE TUTOR'S ROLE:
DEVELOPING AN INFORMED PRACTICE

We believe in the idea of an informed tutoring practice, and we hope this book will serve as a source of information and insight. A tutor who develops a sufficiently broad interpretive frame for understanding his or her own work can apply this knowledge to new situations. In the absence of such a perspective, the tutor has only hit-or-miss, trial-and-error experimentation to rely on—often at the student's expense. On the other hand, tutors who draw on an experience informed by insight and an evolving personal philosophy can bring to the tutoring session the technical skill and creativity needed to teach writing successfully.

This approach suggests a reflective practice, one in which the tutor views rules as guidelines and guidelines as avenues to further refinement of aptitude or "know-how." The "know-how" of good tutors comes from a willingness to reflect on their efforts and to keep learning. Such tutors are eager both to confirm what they do well and to question any practices that impede productive interactions with students. Ultimately, successful tutors are willing to modify their views and procedures as new insights emerge.

The capacity for reconceptualizing is also one of the most significant means for improving writing skills that we as tutors can offer a student. To be a capable writer, a student needs to shift perspective from that of the writer who generated the text to that of an objective reader able to assess his or her own text and its methods of communicating to an audience. Many of the students we work with, though, will have had little experience with reconceptualizing their own writing in this way.

Often students cannot think about their writing in meaningful and productive ways because they are unpracticed at extensive revision. They may see revision as tedious and frustrating. After all, expressing their ideas in writing was probably difficult enough the first time; doing it again in a revised form can seem overwhelming. Knowing how to guide such students through drafting *and* revising can be enormously beneficial to them. By modeling the act of revision, we are demonstrating the process of reflecting on their ideas and written work. We will also be providing the "moral support" that can help sustain motivation. As Muriel Harris, one of the most respected and influential figures in writing center theory and the author of *Teaching One-to-One: The Writing Conference*, says:

> Writers also need another kind of help when revising—some support and encouragement—because the messiness of working and reworking a paper can lead to surprise and dismay as a topic falls apart or changes direction during writing. Novice writers need to learn how to persist, and they need some encouragement to do so. (8)

In emphasizing the interpersonal dimensions of the working relationship between tutor and student, Harris shows how tutoring functions as an assistive process. Tutors have been described as mentors, teachers, therapists, editors, midwives, coaches, grammarmeisters, nurturers, diagnosticians, guides, facilitators, rescuers, advisors, consultants, and allies. Perhaps we are all of these. But primarily, tutors are collaborators: We assist writers in achieving their goals. Among the many traits effective tutors share are good intentions, strong writing and editing skills, flexibility, an eagerness to help, an analytical yet creative mind, a dedication to excellence, good listening skills, an ability to be supportive yet honest, a willingness to work hard, a sense of humor, sensitivity to others, careful judgment, patience, and a dedication to collaborative learning. We need all these traits because solving problems and motivating others are key interpersonal activities in the tutoring process.

THE STAGES OF THE TUTORIAL

While no tutorial is ever exactly like another, most tend to share common patterns. Generally, tutor and student must first establish a working relationship, or mutual understanding, as a basis for collaboration on improving the student's text. Together we set goals for future tutorials and for the direction of the student's independent learning. We have chosen to call these shared activities the pretextual, textual, and posttextual stages of the tutorial.

The Pretextual Stage

In the pretextual stage, tutor and student begin the process of developing the interpersonal relationship that will guide their collaborations. Educational theorists tell us that interpersonal relationships are exceptionally important because they provide a context for interactive learning. In the past, theorists did not place much emphasis on context because they viewed the mind of the learner as an "object" to be filled with information. The method of presenting that information was important, but not the context in which it occurred. But now the mind of the learner is viewed as a process of meaning-making activities. This process is highly influenced by contexts—especially interpersonal ones. As psychologist and learning theorist Richard G. Tiberius writes:

> Effective teachers form relationships that are trustful, open and secure, that involve a minimum of control, are cooperative, and are conducted in a reciprocal, interactive manner. They share control with students and encourage interactions that are determined by mutual agreement. Within such relationships learners are willing to disclose their lack of understanding, rather than hide it from their teachers; learners are more attentive, ask more questions, are more actively engaged. Thus, the better the relationship, the better the interaction; the better the interaction, the better the learning. (1-2)

Most writing center theorists tend to agree with Tiberius in stressing the quality of the interpersonal relationship between tutor and student. For example, in "Freud in the Writing Center: The Psychoanalytics of Tutoring Well" (on p. 43), Christina Murphy maintains that the mutual trust and rapport between tutor and student determines how successful the tutorial as a whole will be. To achieve this level of reciprocal learning, Murphy contends, tutors often need to break through psychological barriers that might otherwise impede collaboration. In "Humor and the Serious Tutor" (on p. 48), Steve Sherwood points out that many students are intimidated by the tutorial itself, fearing another person's judgment of their work and thus feeling anxious, insecure, and filled with self-doubt. Sherwood discusses humor as one approach the tutor can draw on to ease the student's tension and encourage a deeper involvement in the learning process.

In establishing an interpersonal relationship, the tutor must respond to various personality and learning styles and be sensitive to differences in gender, age, ethnicity, cultural and educational backgrounds, and attitudes toward writing. The ways in which individuals process information must always be taken into account, too, since people tend to interpret, understand, and evaluate ideas in diverse ways. Consequently, tutors need to engage in what Harris calls "perception checking" or "guessing the student's basic message and asking for affirmation of that guess" (57). In a similar vein, Emily Meyer and Louise Z. Smith claim that tutors "must listen carefully to distinguish underlying meanings in writers' comments" (9) and work diligently to be certain that those meanings are understood. Tutors should strive to understand, not judge, the student and to recognize the importance of the student's problems and feelings. Students vary in levels of autonomy, sensitivity to criticism, ego strength, personal maturity, motivation, and perseverance. Relating to the student as an individual and empathizing with his or her particular personality and character traits will go a long way toward forming a special trust, one that provides the motivation, energy, and direction for the tutorial itself.

When individuals choose to work together, their transactions should be based on a shared dialogue. Too often collaborations that seem democratic may actually be autocratic and controlling, as Andrea Lunsford indicates in her essay. Sometimes in a tutorial we need to overcome an assumed hierarchy of power, with the tutor in command and the student acting as a subservient petitioner. A good question for tutors to ask ourselves is, "Who has the power in the collaboration and how is that power used?" Are we, for example, truly interested in what the student has to say, or are we too quick to announce our opinions? Are we acting as collaborators or as authority figures? Do our comments invite responses and show respect for the student's ideas, or do they foreclose further interaction and leave the student feeling intimidated? As Carol Severino points out, collaboration can be analyzed rhetorically by considering how the agenda for the conference is decided, the length of each person's contributions to the discussions, and the rhetorical functions of verbal exchanges and of body language (56). All of these dimensions are available for your investigation during tutorials. Self-reflection can assist you in assessing your interpersonal transactions and in responding to students' needs.

In "'Whispers of Coming and Going': Lessons from Fannie" (on p. 55), Anne DiPardo discusses another dimension of interpersonal sensitivity—an appreciation of diversity. The students you tutor will come from different backgrounds, often different cultures. Their ways of looking at the world and interpreting experience may be strikingly different from yours, though equally valid. As DiPardo notes, we can serve students best by avoiding stereotypical and preconceived ideas and by being curious about how their ways of thinking differ from ours. Appreciating the multiplicity of perspectives encountered among students will add to our skill as tutors. As examples of this diversity, consider the following scenarios based on actual writing center interactions.

Darren and Yaroslav Darren worked with Yaroslav, a Russian student, on an assignment for his composition class to write a letter to the editor to argue against changes in governmental policies. From their initial conversations, Darren saw that Yaroslav was a bright, articulate, and highly motivated student. Yet there seemed to be a problem. Yaroslav was reluctant to discuss the requirements of the assignment and to work with Darren toward a rudimentary outline or draft.

Darren was patient and continued to ask Yaroslav questions related to the assignment. Did he understand the requirements of a paper that asked for a writer to take a stand on an issue? Had he ever written a similar paper before? With that question, Yaroslav suddenly became very animated. "In my country," he said, "you do not write letters to the editor to complain about the government. You could be imprisoned for such an act of defiance."

Thus, Darren discovered that the issues that had made the tutorial difficult to that point did not result from Yaroslav's weaknesses as a writer or from a lack of motivation to complete his assignment. Rather, they arose from a cultural difference that had to do with the freedom of an individual to be politically active in one society versus another.

Had Darren not patiently addressed the resistance he sensed in Yaroslav, he might have merely assumed that Yaroslav was scattered, disorganized, or not ready to begin and sent him off to work on his own for awhile. As it turned out, his sensitivity created a supportive atmosphere in which Yaroslav was able to talk through his fears and realize that what would be an unimaginable and terrifying act in his culture was an everyday, safe occurrence in Darren's culture. Darren encouraged Yaroslav to shift perspectives and imagine the political freedom to express negative opinions about governmental policies. What would this be like? What actions would Yaroslav want to take? What would he most want to change politically? Eventually, because Darren had made his discussions with Yaroslav nonjudgmental and nonthreatening, Yaroslav began the process of drafting his essay. The understanding Darren and Yaroslav had achieved made the tutorial successful.

Laura and Ted Laura worked with Ted in a number of tutorials before he confided in her that he had a learning disability. He showed her his letter of accommodation from the coordinator for academic services and talked about how he usually could do well on tests if given a little extra time. Laura was surprised to discover that Ted had a learning disability. At that moment, in thinking about Ted in a new light, she realized that she had held a stereotypical view of students with learning disabilities as "slower" than "normal" students. Yet here was Ted, who was so hard-working and was zipping through his computer science courses with high grades. He didn't seem "slow" at all. In fact, he seemed bright and talented.

"I can't read," Ted said, laughing. "At least not the way you do. I have dyslexia. Letters kind of tumble around on the page—you know, upside down, backwards, the whole bit. But if I take my time and work with my colors, I can manage pretty well."

When Ted mentioned his colors, a lot became clear to Laura. She remembered the way Ted marked up his drafts in highlighter colors of green, yellow, pink, and orange. When they talked, Ted always took notes and then highlighted sections of the notes in the various colors.

Laura didn't think much about it at the time. She assumed that Ted had his own way of organizing his work. Now, as Ted explained his system, she realized that Ted was using his enormous visual memory to compensate for his difficulties in processing symbols. Ted could literally "see" his paper in his mind once he had the paper coded to show its organization and to emphasize certain stylistic techniques.

"It's all about neurological processing," he said. "Some of us do it differently."

At that moment, Laura felt embarrassed. She remembered the popular phrase on her campus that students with learning disabilities were not "disabled" but "differently abled." She realized that she had never really understood that phrase as more than a slogan. Now Ted had made that phrase real for her. He was exceptionally "abled," and he went about his learning and information processing in a different way. She admired his motivation and drive. Ted had to work many times harder and longer than the "normal" student, yet he persevered and actually became quite creative in finding new ways to learn and to succeed.

"You know, I was kind of hesitant to tell you I had a learning disability," Ted said. "Sometimes people can't handle it. They freak out and start treating you differently, or they assume you're a basket case and start doing everything for you. Or worse yet, they start distancing themselves from you, like you're some kind of freak they just can't cope with. It's no fun."

"I can imagine," Laura said.

"But I wanted to be honest," Ted said. "I wanted you to know me for who I am. And I wanted to thank you."

Laura was a bit surprised.

"You've always been very patient with me. When I needed something explained more than once, you always would. You went through your explanations step by step, and that helped me a lot. Like I said, I can usually do pretty well if I have a little extra time—and a little extra encouragement."

When Laura reviewed her tutorials with her peer tutoring coordinator, she told him she was dismayed to discover how unenlightened her attitude toward students with learning disabilities was.

"I just had a superficial knowledge," she said. "And lots of stereotypical thinking. I really learned a lot from Ted about encouraging people to speak openly about themselves and about not prejudging anybody."

Laura's tutorials with Ted confirm Shoshana Beth Konstant's views in "Multi-sensory Tutoring for Multi-sensory Learners" (on p. 108). Konstant believes that tutors can best work with students who have learning disabilities by discovering and encouraging each student's own way of processing information. Doing so allows the tutor to provide commentary relevant to the student's particular learning style.

Paul and Leonard Leonard had been the manager of a trucking company for over twenty years before being laid off. Now he was returning to the university to get a degree in engineering and pursue another career. Leonard was highly motivated, organized, and very sure of his abilities—except when it came to expressing himself in writing.

"I haven't had an English class in about thirty years," he said to Paul during their first tutorial. "Now I have to write a personal essay for my

composition class, and I'm not even sure what a personal essay is. All I
know is I have to write something about my experiences, and I can't seem
to get started."

"Are you experiencing writer's block?" Paul asked.

"I guess I am."

"Are you kind of a perfectionist? I mean, do you expect to get everything right the first time?"

Leonard nodded. "When you're in the trucking business, you'd better
get it right the first time."

"I'm sure that's true, but did it always work out that way?"

After some thought, Leonard conceded that the more complex the task, the
greater the probability of error. As they talked, Paul sensed that Leonard liked
his world to be clear-cut—simple, neat, and organized. Paul realized his first
priority was showing Leonard that the writing task could be more manageable
than it seemed, but that Leonard would still probably experience setbacks along
the way. He explained the drafting and revision stages. He also explained that
most writers feel some measure of self-doubt, especially in the early stages of
coming up with ideas and finding a way to express them.

Paul said, "It seems to me that, since you were in the trucking business, you should have a lot of material for writing a personal essay."

Leonard's face brightened. "You mean I could write about my old job?"

"Sure. Why not? That's personal, isn't it?"

"Yeah, very." Leonard thought for a moment. "Oh I see," he said.
"Personal—like from my life."

Paul asked Leonard, "If you were going to write about your old job,
what would you want a reader to know?"

"The first thing I'd want to tell them is that you can work for a
company for twenty years, do your best and put your life's blood into the
business, but, when times get tough, you get the ax anyway."

"Could we set this up as a scene? You know, like a story—a narrative—so
that people could experience this from your point of view?"

As the two discussed options for the essay, Paul suggested the idea of beginning the narrative with strong visual imagery and perhaps some dialogue. This
appealed to Leonard because his last conversation with his ex-boss was still
fresh in his mind. As he told Paul, it was raining and bitterly cold the night he
lost his job. He had driven to the dispatch office and brought his thermos of
coffee in from the car. He still remembered how cold the metal thermos had
felt, even after he had stepped into the warm office. Then he saw his boss's
pained expression. Even though Leonard suspected what was coming, he still
couldn't believe it when it happened.

"What you've just told me is very vivid," Paul said. "I can feel the
coldness of the thermos, too. Why don't we begin with that scene and
perhaps the conversation you and your boss had that night?"

Leonard liked this approach and began brainstorming with Paul to come up with more details he could include. In a short while, the two had begun work on a preliminary outline, and the idea of a personal essay no longer seemed so mysterious or intimidating to Leonard.

Paul helped to build Leonard's confidence as a writer by making him aware of competencies he already had. He pointed out to Leonard how visual his descriptions were and how he could use this talent to his advantage in a personal essay. He also helped Leonard to see that his past experiences were relevant now.

Paul's work with Leonard affirms Cynthia Haynes-Burton's position in "'Thirty-something' Students: Concerning Transitions in the Writing Center" (on p. 103) that tutoring nontraditional students often involves "showing them how to channel the confidence they possess in other areas of their life and apply it to writing problems." Tiberius echoes this same idea in stating that "the best we can do to help students learn is to connect what we say to their previous experience and knowledge" (1).

Each of these tutorials demonstrates the power of the interpersonal relationship to accommodate diversity, foster communication, and allow the student to take positive action. In this supportive environment,

- The tutor can help reduce the student's anxieties, self-doubts, and insecurities that can lead to writer's block, a sense of failure, and poor self-esteem.
- The tutor can help the student to break a writing project of intimidating size and scope into smaller pieces (or stages) that the student can more easily manage.
- The student can get his or her ideas out in the open where they can be reacted to, examined, discussed, clarified, tested, and, if necessary, revised.
- The student has an opportunity to practice collaborative problem solving with an experienced writer who has the student's best interest in mind.
- The student can observe, reflect upon, and perhaps internalize the invention processes of the tutor.

Ultimately, a positive interpersonal relationship built in the pretextual stage allows for a fluid transition to a consideration of the student's text.

The Textual Stage

Students bring to the writing center the type of textual problems faced by writers at all levels of ability. They suffer from writer's block or from not knowing when to stop writing; they have something they want to say but can't quite put into words; or their most beloved passages are incomprehensible to their readers. In addition, they often have problems with grammar, style, syntax, logic, organization, tone, diction, and focus. To find solutions that remain true to the student's writing style and intent, a tutor must learn to address the student's needs while also creating a collaborative space within which confidence and skills can flourish.

The goal of most tutors is to assist students in making long-term improvements in their writing. In "Provocative Revision" (on p. 71) Toby Fulwiler argues that teaching writers how to improve involves teaching them how to revise, saying that "revision is the primary way that both thinking and writing evolve, mature, and improve." Many students, though, identify tutoring with proofreading, or simple error detection and correction. They may be primarily interested in making sure their papers are grammatically and mechanically correct and only secondarily interested in your assessment of the quality of their ideas and the effectiveness of their organization. This attitude can put tutor and student at cross purposes, creating a central dilemma for the tutor about how much to intervene in the student's overall writing processes. In essence, should we serve as editors of basic errors or as commentators on larger concerns when critiquing a student's writing and offering assistance?

This dilemma arises in nearly all tutoring situations. As you will see in Brooks's essay, some tutors attempt to resolve this dilemma by taking a hands-off, or *minimalist*, approach to the text. They focus on global issues such as thesis, structure, diction, tone, and the logical development of ideas. Students read their texts aloud; the tutor comments. As commentators, minimalist tutors assist students in solving their own problems. They ask heuristic questions— questions that encourage students to analyze their work and seek solutions to the difficulties the writing presents. Questions such as "Are you aware of the many simple sentences you use throughout your essay and the monotonous effect this can produce for a reader?" or "Have you thought about reorganizing your ideas along another line?" might prove more beneficial to a student's growth as a writer than simply correcting errors and sending the student off to reproduce a clean, error-free copy to hand in to the teacher. Minimalist tutors believe that proofreading and editing must be understood within the broader context of the writing process. Basic grammatical or mechanical errors may be symptomatic of deeper problems with text development, and just correcting those errors for the student will not resolve the larger issues.

Minimalist tutoring can present its own set of difficulties, however. A tutor who listens to a student read a text aloud and does not look at the text might not be able to detect certain types of formal errors that may affect meaning. For example, the sentence "The auditors role is to evaluate financial statements and certify that the statements have been fairly presented without material error" sounds correct when read aloud. But when viewed as a written text, the sentence's apostrophe error becomes apparent.

The difference between spoken and written text is further demonstrated by the interaction between Steve, a tutor, and Shafik, an ESL student who came to the writing center with a paper on the Muslim religion. Shafik asked for help in expressing his ideas clearly. Steve had him read his paper aloud and listened to the most polished, well-organized essay he had come across in weeks.

"Your ideas seem clear enough to me," Steve said.

"When I speak them, yes," Shafik said as he handed Steve the manuscript, "but I have a slight problem with English grammar."

It turned out that Shafik's essay was a single paragraph, ten pages long, punctuated haphazardly, with a comma roughly every fifty words and a period every hundred. Shafik's case points to at least one problem a strictly minimalist approach can lead to. It can fail to help students like Shafik, whose overall structure, clarity of expression, and development of ideas are just fine, but whose otherwise eloquently phrased sentences need grammatical editing. In "Rethinking Writing Center Conferencing Strategies for the ESL Writer" (on p. 96), Judith K. Powers calls attention to the limitations of minimalist tutoring for ESL students like Shafik:

> Neither reading aloud nor editing by ear appears to work for the majority of ESL writers. . . . Since they have no inner editor prompting them to stop and raise questions, we are likely to adjust our technique to their needs and discover we are locating errors for ESL writers in a way that looks very much like editing.

Not all tutors, however, object to editing a student's text. Some consider modeling this part of the revision process for the student a significant aid to comprehension. In "Collaboration and Ethics in Writing Center Pedagogy" (on p. 88), Irene Lurkis Clark suggests that some students might benefit from the experience of watching a tutor edit their text. Clark refers to "a respected, well-published professor" she knows who gives credit for his eloquent writing style to a tutor in Britain who "would cross out any awkward sentences he found and replace them with more felicitous wording. As a student, [Clark's colleague] would faithfully imitate the style and language of his tutor, and, eventually, the tutor's suggestions became part of his own style." Clark maintains that, if this tutor had not worked with her colleague on a one-to-one basis, carefully and constructively pointing out errors and showing how corrections could be made, the colleague's writing style might not have developed as fully. Then again, perhaps the colleague was an exceptional student with a quick mind, eager to learn and ready to assimilate lessons. A less motivated, less interested student might have paid little attention to the reasons for the corrections and simply rewritten them as his or her own. For this kind of student, having a tutor correct these basic errors might simply have served as a convenient means toward the goal of an error-free paper. Perhaps such a student would have benefited more from a tutor who adopted the role of commentator.

For many tutors, the dilemma of how much help to give can be personally troubling. The natural tendency to be helpful and supportive may conflict with a sense that doing too much of the student's work will not produce the desired result of improving his or her writing abilities and critical-thinking skills. A related dilemma is the question of how candid to be in critiquing a student's work. Some students are mature enough to deal with having their work critiqued. Other students are far more fragile. As Peter Elbow says in *Writing with Power*, "Some people are terrified no matter how friendly the audience is, while others are not intimidated even by sharks" (184-85). With the complex of problems, needs, ego strengths, and personality styles students bring to the tutoring situation, what courses of action should the tutor pursue to be effective? The following ideas might prove helpful:

- *Give a candid opinion of the strengths and weaknesses of the work in progress; in the process, be sensitive to the student's reactions.* Such candor can be difficult, but honesty about the problems you detect with the reasoning, structure, or content of an essay is essential for improvement. This is not to say that criticism doesn't hurt. It sometimes does. But anything short of a truthful—but also sensitive—appraisal is a betrayal of the student's trust.
- *Suggest ways to enhance the strengths and minimize the weaknesses in the student's writing.* A tutorial that focuses exclusively, or even primarily, on weaknesses can leave a student feeling demoralized. Noting strengths and achievements in the writing can build a student's confidence and set the tone for comments and suggestions that follow.
- *Recognize that every text and every writer is a work in progress.* Writers progress at different levels, but they do progress—in part because they acquire greater intellectual maturity, and in part because writing is an ongoing learning experience. Writers learn to be better writers by striving to improve. The issue is not whether they will make mistakes—because they will; the issue is whether they will learn from those mistakes or be defeated by them. Here the tutor can be instrumental. As a supportive ally and a candid critic, a tutor can encourage progress by fostering potential.

The Posttextual Stage

The posttextual stage has two major functions: it provides a sense of closure for the tutorial and it offers a *template*, or model, for future learning experiences. The most helpful tutorials do not simply "end"; they are brought to a satisfactory conclusion. Tutor and student seek an overview that brings the strategic insights of the tutorial into focus and clarifies what work still remains to be done. Ultimately, this perspective contributes to the student's ease in working with a tutor and makes future tutoring sessions seem natural extensions of an ongoing learning process.

This concluding stage also contributes to students' feelings of empowerment, providing them with the confidence they need to take the insights they have gained and apply them in new writing situations. In this regard, the concluding stage requires that you encourage self-motivated and independent learning styles for the student as a way of preventing the student from becoming overdependent on your help. You can accomplish this objective in several ways: first, by leaving the student with a clear sense of where to go from here; second, by letting the student know that revision is well within the limits of his or her abilities; third, by providing a perceptive audience for the student's future work; and fourth, by refusing to be satisfied with anything less than the student's best effort. Not all students will respond to your demands for their best work. Those who do will grow as a result of learning to push themselves rather than settling for the easy solution. Eventually, if they internalize these expectations, they can become their own best audience.

As an example of a tutorial that was successful in encouraging independent learning, consider Barbara, a student who came to the writing center with a paper about William Faulkner's *Sanctuary*. During the initial "reading" of the student to establish a working relationship, Steve, the tutor, interviewed Barbara to learn a number of key pieces of information. For instance, Barbara told Steve that her professor had refused to grade her essay, saying that she needed help at all stages of her writing. Steve also learned that Barbara was a mother of three who had quit college as a sophomore nine years earlier and was now trying to pick up where she had left off. Barbara admitted she was feeling discouraged, saying, "It's been ten years since I've taken a writing course, and I've lost the knack. Anyway, my professor has a problem with the way I write. I'm worried about this paper," she said, "but I'm more worried about what's going to happen next year if I don't improve my writing."

Barbara moved the tutorial into the textual stage by showing Steve a heavily marked-up manuscript. "My teacher says I need to make a point and that I have problems with sentence structure," she said. She read her essay aloud, and Steve primarily noted rough transitions and a general lack of organization. In the essay, Barbara tended to repeat herself, to think in circles rather than systematically developing her main idea. Even so, Steve told Barbara that, circular or not, her ideas were good, that she had something interesting to say on Faulkner's motives for writing about particular characters. Together, they worked out a tentative essay structure. Since Barbara's main stylistic and mechanical errors were short, choppy sentences, errors of diction, and sentence fragments, Steve also went over individual sentences, asking Barbara to add the necessary elements.

Toward the end of the tutorial, Steve reviewed what they had accomplished, gave Barbara some words of encouragement, and then sent her away to write. Three days later, Barbara returned. Her paper had taken a new direction, and, though the paper occasionally wandered off the point, Steve felt it might work with some adjustments. He encouraged Barbara to rewrite along the lines they had discussed.

Steve did not see Barbara for over a week; then she returned to say she had received a B+ on the essay. "The best thing is, I did most of the work on my own," she said proudly. She was feeling independent and ready to face the challenges of future assignments. Through discussion, questioning, and being open both to small corrections and major changes in thinking, Barbara had gained a sense of the composing process.

Stimulating independent learning is an important aspect of the tutoring process and is the primary objective of the posttextual stage. When the posttextual stage is successful, students work to develop their own strengths separately from those of the tutor, taking what they can from the more experienced member of the relationship and adding this knowledge to an already existing repertoire of technique and understanding. In so doing, they build a knowledge indebted to, but independent of, their tutor's. As Wallace Stegner, a noted author and creative writing teacher, says, "Something unpredictable has happened in your head or on your typewriter, and no teacher did it—though a teacher may have helped it along" (19).

As a tutor, you can help foster independent learning and writing by

- letting students do what they can for themselves
- reminding students of any challenges they have conquered on their own or with minimal help
- recognizing and praising any steps they take toward independence in their writing
- refusing to let students credit you with their successes
- letting them know that, while you value their increasing independence, you will gladly help them cope with future challenges they might feel unable to face alone.

As Murphy states, ". . . a good tutor function[s] to awaken individuals to their potentials and to channel their creative energies toward self-enhancing ends."

ON BECOMING AN EFFECTIVE TUTOR

We hope that investigating the tutoring process from a number of perspectives has revealed to you its philosophical complexity, interpersonal richness, and educational significance. We also hope that it has intensified both your desire to be a tutor and your willingness to continue learning how to improve your craft. Actually, tutoring is more than a craft; it is also an art form—one that will continue to evolve as you acquire more experience and wisdom. Everyone who has ever tutored has stood where you stand now—at the beginning of the journey into tutoring or a little bit farther down the road. We assume you have started on that journey because you believe in the value of your work as a tutor. That value is often hard to measure in a quantitative sense, but it is exceptionally easy to experience as personal satisfaction when the work you do is helpful to another. We believe that assisting others is best achieved in an informed practice that blends experience, theory, and reflection. We hope this sourcebook will assist you in developing a philosophy and style of your own and, ultimately, in achieving your full potential as a tutor.

Works Cited

Elbow, Peter. *Writing with Power: Techniques for Mastering the Writing Process*. New York: Oxford UP, 1981.

Harris, Muriel. *Teaching One-to-One: The Writing Conference*. Urbana: NCTE, 1986.

Meyer, Emily, and Louise Z. Smith. *The Practical Tutor*. New York: Oxford UP, 1987.

Severino, Carol. "Rhetorically Analyzing Collaboration(s)." *The Writing Center Journal* 13.1 (1992): 53–64.

Stegner, Wallace. *On the Teaching of Creative Writing.* Hanover: UP of New England, 1988.
Tiberius, Richard G. "The Why of Teacher/Student Relationships." *Teaching Effectiveness: Toward the Best in the Academy* 6.1 (1994-95): 1-2.

PART

II

Readings:
Entering the Professional Conversation

This group of essays introduces you to many of the ideas and issues currently defining the practice of tutoring. In a sense, it provides a body of knowledge about the function of tutoring within the broader context of educational theory.

The theorists and practitioners whose work is presented here examine the role of the tutor, speculate upon the types of language and instructional transactions that occur in tutorials, consider tutoring in relation to current ideas about composition instruction, and discuss tutoring's significance to multicultural issues. Their essays have been grouped according to the following common concerns: (1) theoretical constructs that underlie instruction in the writing center; (2) interpersonal dynamics of tutoring; (3) techniques for critiquing students' texts; and (4) affirming diversity.

Stephen M. North's "The Idea of a Writing Center" and Andrea Lunsford's "Collaboration, Control, and the Idea of a Writing Center" examine the paradigms, or models, of composition instruction that shape writing center tutorials. As discussed in the previous chapter, such paradigms include current traditional rhetoric, expressivism, and social constructionism. In responding to the constraints of current traditional rhetoric, North rejects the stereotypical image of the writing center as a "fix-it shop" and "skills center" for remediation. Instead, he validates the principles of expressivism in viewing the writing center as an instructional site in which "the object is to make sure that writers, and not necessarily their texts, are what get changed by instruction." As tutors, "our job is to produce better writers, not better writing," North claims, moving the focus of writing center instruction from the text to the writer. Lunsford provides an overview of how writing centers have progressed from the "storehouses" of current traditional rhetoric, to the "garrets" of expressivism, to the "Burkean parlors" of social constructionism. Like North, she finds limited value in the emphases of current traditional rhetoric, but she also challenges expressivism's belief in the interiority of knowledge and its romantic view of the writer as a solitary creator.

While North and Lunsford consider the *epistemological*, or knowledge-related, issues that define the philosophical boundaries of writing center tutorials, Christina Murphy in "Freud in the Writing Center: The Psychoanalytics of Tutoring Well," Steve Sherwood in "Humor and the Serious Tutor" and Anne

DiPardo in "'Whispers of Coming and Going': Lessons from Fannie" examine the interpersonal dynamics involved in the tutor's role. Murphy explores the quality and importance of the interpersonal relationships tutors build with students by comparing such relationships to those psychoanalysts develop with their clients; according to Murphy, "a good psychoanalyst and a good tutor both function to awaken individuals to their potentials and to channel their creative energies toward self-enhancing ends." Reinforcing the emphasis Murphy places on the bond between tutor and student, Sherwood contends that tutors can "encourage an enlightened, collaborative environment in writing centers . . . through the intelligent and humane use of humor." As he states, "A writing center without laughter can be a grim, fearful place, and we must not disregard the role humor can play in facilitating interactive learning." DiPardo discusses the tutor-student relationship in terms of multicultural sensitivity, emphasizing how tutors can facilitate successful interactions with students from diverse cultural backgrounds. She tells of Fannie, a Native American student, and of the dialogues through which Fannie and her tutor negotiated a working relationship sensitive to the "hidden corners" of a student's cultural heritage. As DiPardo states, "Often placed on the front lines of efforts to provide respectful, insightful attention to these students' diverse struggles with academic discourse, writing tutors likewise occupy multiple roles, remaining learners even while emerging as teachers, perenially searching for a suitable social stance. . . ."

Toby Fulwiler in "Provocative Revision," Jeff Brooks in "Minimalist Tutoring: Making the Student Do All the Work," and Irene Lurkis Clark in "Collaboration and Ethics in Writing Center Pedagogy" describe the tutor's assistive role in augmenting the student's understanding of the writing process. Fulwiler emphasizes revision, pointing out that "teaching writing is teaching re-writing." He provides a model for teaching the revision process so that tutors can help writers understand that "re-seeing writing in a different form is . . . generative, liberating, and fun." Clark agrees with Fulwiler's view that teaching revision is a major component of tutoring as an assistive process. She contends that modeling the revision process for a student through a careful editing of the student's work can be especially instructive. Brooks, on the other hand, argues against a tutor's intervening directly by editing the student's text; instead, he advocates "minimalist" tutoring, in which the tutor is a commentator rather than an editor. By discussing the areas of the student's writing that need improvement and by examining the student's options for revision, the tutor fulfills an important and highly individualized instructional role. As Brooks indicates, "Fixing flawed papers is easy; showing the students how to fix their papers is complex and difficult."

Judith K. Powers in "Rethinking Writing Center Conferencing: Strategies for the ESL Writer," Shoshana Beth Konstant in "Multi-sensory Tutoring for Multi-sensory Learners," and Cynthia Haynes-Burton in "'Thirty-something' Students: Concerning Transitions in the Writing Center" explore through case histories and narrative examples the value of tutoring as a one-to-one, individual process. These three writers also focus on the educational and sociocultural backgrounds of multicultural and nontraditional students, examining how these dimensions influence tutorials. Powers explores the limitations of tutoring models that are not sensitive to cultural values and that are instead shaped more to the experiences of native writers. Many tutorial strategies, such as having the student read a paper aloud to detect problem areas, presume a sensitivity to English that nonnative writers often do not possess. Even attitudes toward the student-tutor relationship may differ among cultures, and "attempts . . . to play off such experience in devising collaborative strategies are likely to fail," Powers contends. Konstant discusses the ways in which students with learning disabilities process information through visual, auditory, and kinesthetic channels and how tutors should adapt their instruction to reinforce each student's primary mode of learning. She asks, "Why spend twenty minutes verbally explaining something to a visual learner? Why not teach to the student's strengths?" Haynes-Burton develops a perspective similar to Powers's views in considering the needs of nontraditional students. She, too, questions whether commonly accepted models of the tutoring process have as great a relevance for nontraditional students whose life experiences and capabilities tend to differ from those of traditional students.

Because these authors discuss the tutoring process and explore the central issues concerning writing center practices in clear and helpful terms, their essays can provide an initiation into the field for novice tutors while also reminding experienced tutors of the complexity and richness of their work. Reading essays like these can help tutors avoid what DiPardo calls "a vision of 'collaboration' that casts it as a set of techniques rather than a new way to think about teaching and learning . . . a fossilized creed, a shield against more fundamental concerns." Instead, as informed tutors, aware of the ongoing professional conversation that contributes to defining writing center practice, they can set about developing their own philosophies of tutoring.

THEORETICAL CONSTRUCTS

The Idea of a Writing Center

Stephen M. North _____

STATE UNIVERSITY OF NEW YORK AT ALBANY

Stephen M. North contends that many students, writing instructors, and faculty in other disciplines do not understand the role of the writing center. They tend to view the writing center as a "skills center" or "fix-it shop" for grammar correction and writer remediation rather than as a place of active learning and student enrichment. North directs tutors toward examining a student's text as an indicator of the processes that produced it, rather than as a product that must be reworked to meet accepted standards of form and correctness. In this fashion, and in his assertion that tutoring should be "student-centered" rather than text-oriented, he endorses the primary tenets of expressivism in writing center pedagogy. A classic essay, frequently quoted and cited in writing center scholarship, "The Idea of a Writing Center" is important for tutors in contrasting two models of writing center instruction—one that stresses "the correction of textual problems" and another that focuses on the writer's intellectual and personal involvement in the creation of texts. North's essay is also important for its examination of the tutor's role within a "student-centered" pedagogy in which the writing center's "primary responsibility" and "only reason for being" is "to talk to writers." This essay originally appeared in 1984 in College English.

THIS IS AN ESSAY THAT BEGAN out of frustration. Despite the reference to writing centers in the title, it is not addressed to a writing center audience but to what is, for my purposes, just the opposite: those not involved with writing centers. Do not exclude yourself from this group just because you know that writing centers (or labs or clinics or places or however you think of them) exist; "involved" here means having directed such a place, having worked there for a minimum of 100 hours, or, at the very least, having talked about writing of your own there for five or more hours. The source of my frustration? Ignorance: the members of my profession, my colleagues, people I might see at MLA or CCCC or read in the pages of *College English*, do not understand what I do. They do not understand what does happen, what can happen, in a writing center.

Let me be clear here. Misunderstanding is something one expects—and almost gets used to—in the writing center business. The new faculty member in our writing-across-the-curriculum program, for example, who sends his students to get their papers "cleaned up" in the Writing Center before they hand them in; the occasional student who tosses her paper on our reception desk, announcing that she'll "pick it up in an hour"; even the well-intentioned administrators who are so happy that we deal with "skills" or "fundamentals" or, to use the word that seems to subsume all others, "grammar" (or usually "GRAMMAR")—these are fairly predictable. But from people in English departments, people well trained in the complex relationship between writer and text, so painfully aware, if only from the composing of dissertations and theses, how lonely and difficult writing can be, I expect more. And I am generally disappointed.

What makes the situation particularly frustrating is that so many such people will vehemently claim that they do, *really*, understand the idea of a writing center. The non-English faculty, the students, the administrators—they may not understand what a writing center is or does, but they have no investment in their ignorance, and can often be educated. But in English departments this second layer of ignorance, this false sense of knowing, makes it doubly hard to get a message through. Indeed, even as you read now, you may be dismissing my argument as the ritual plaint of a "remedial" teacher begging for respectability, the product of a kind of professional paranoia. But while I might admit that there are elements of such a plaint involved—no one likes not to be understood—there is a good deal more at stake. For in coming to terms with this ignorance, I have discovered that it is only a symptom of a much deeper, more serious problem. As a profession I think we are holding on tightly to attitudes and beliefs about the teaching and learning of writing that we thought we had left behind. In fact, my central contention—in the first half of this essay, anyway—is that the failure or inability of the bulk of the English teaching profession, including even those most ardent spokespersons of the so-called "revolution" in the teaching of writing, to perceive the idea of a writing center suggests that, for all our noise and bother about composition, we have fundamentally changed very little.

Let me begin by citing a couple of typical manifestations of this ignorance from close to home. Our writing center has been open for seven years. During that time we have changed our philosophy a little bit as a result of lessons learned from experience, but for the most part we have always been open to anybody in the university community, worked with writers at any time during the composing of a given piece of writing, and dealt with whole pieces of discourse, and not exercises on what might be construed as "subskills" (spelling, punctuation, etc.) outside of the context of the writer's work.

We have delivered the message about what we do to the university generally, and the English department in particular, in a number of ways: letters, flyers, posters, class presentations, information booths, and so on. And, as long as there has been a writing committee, advisory to the director of the writing program, we have sent at least one representative. So it is all the more surprising, and disheartening, that the text for our writing program flyer, composed and approved by that committee, should read as follows:

> The University houses the Center for Writing, founded in 1978 to sponsor the interdisciplinary study of writing. Among its projects are a series of summer institutes for area teachers of writing, a resource center for writers and teachers of writing, *and a tutorial facility for those with special problems in composition.* (My emphasis)

I don't know, quite frankly, how that copy got past me. What are these "special problems"? What would constitute a regular problem, and why wouldn't we talk to the owner of one? Is this hint of pathology, in some mysterious way, a good marketing ploy?

But that's only the beginning. Let me cite another, in many ways more common and painful instance. As a member, recently, of a doctoral examination committee, I conducted an oral in composition theory and practice. One of the candidate's areas of concentration was writing centers, so as part of the exam I gave her a piece of student writing and asked her to play tutor to my student. The session went well enough, but afterward, as we evaluated the entire exam, one of my fellow examiners—a longtime colleague and friend—said that, while the candidate handled the tutoring nicely, he was surprised that the student who had written the paper would have bothered with the Writing Center in the first place. He would not recommend a student to the Center, he said, "unless there were something like twenty-five errors per page."

People make similar remarks all the time, stopping me or members of my staff in the halls, or calling us into offices, to discuss—in hushed tones, frequently—their current "impossible" or difficult students. There was a time, I will confess, when I let my frustration get the better of me. I would be more or less combative, confrontational, challenging the instructor's often well-intentioned but not very useful "diagnosis." We no longer bother with such confrontations; they never worked very well, and they risk undermining the genuine compassion our teachers have for the students they single out. Nevertheless, their behavior makes it clear that for them, a writing center is to illiteracy what a cross between Lourdes and a hospice would be to serious illness: one goes there hoping for miracles, but ready to face the inevitable. In their minds, clearly, writers fall into three fairly distinct groups: the talented, the average, and the others; and the Writing Center's only logical *raison d'etre* must be to handle those others—those, as the flyer proclaims, with "special problems."

Mine is not, of course, the only English department in which such misconceptions are rife. One comes away from any large meeting of writing center people laden with similar horror stories. And in at least one case, a member of such a department—Malcolm Hayward of the Indiana University of Pennsylvania—decided formally to explore and document his faculty's perceptions of the center, and to compare them with the views the center's staff held.[1] His aim, in a two-part survey of both groups, was to determine, first, which goals each group deemed most important in the teaching of writing; and second, what role they thought the writing center ought to play in that teaching, which goals it ought to concern itself with.

Happily, the writing center faculty and the center staff agreed on what the primary goals in teaching writing should be (in the terms offered by Hayward's questionnaire): the development of general patterns of thinking and writing. Unhappily, the two groups disagreed rather sharply about the reasons for referring students to the center. For faculty members the two primary criteria were grammar and punctuation. Tutors, on the other hand, ranked organization "as by far the single most important factor for referral," followed rather distantly by paragraphing, grammar, and style. In short, Hayward's survey reveals the same kind of misunderstanding on his campus that I find so frustrating on my own: the idea that a writing center can only be some sort of skills center, a fix-it shop.

Now if this were just a matter of local misunderstanding, if Hayward and I could straighten it out with a few workshops or lectures, maybe I wouldn't need to write this essay for a public forum. But that is not the case. For whatever reasons writing centers have gotten mostly this kind of press, have been represented—or misrepresented—more often as fix-it shops than in any other way, and in some fairly influential places. Consider, for example, this passage from Barbara E. Fassler Walvoord's *Helping Students Write Well: A Guide for Teachers in All Disciplines* (New York: Modern Language Association, 1981). What makes it particularly odd, at least in terms of my argument, is that Professor Walvoord's book, in many other ways, offers to faculty the kind of perspective on writing (writing as a complex process, writing as a way of learning) that I might offer myself. Yet here she is on writing centers:

> If you are very short of time, if you think you are not skilled enough to deal with mechanical problems, or if you have a number of students with serious difficulties, you may wish to let the skills center carry the ball for mechanics and spend your time on other kinds of writing and learning problems. (p. 63)

Don't be misled by Professor Walvoord's use of the "skills center" label; in her index the entry for "Writing centers" reads "See skills centers"—precisely the kind of interchangeable terminology I find so abhorrent. On the other hand, to do Professor Walvoord justice, she does recommend that teachers become "at least generally aware of how your skills center works with students, what its basic philosophy is, and what goals it sets for the students in your class," but it seems to me that she has already restricted the possible scope of such a philosophy pretty severely: "deal with mechanical problems"? "carry the ball for mechanics"?

Still, as puzzling and troubling as it is to see Professor Walvoord publishing misinformation about writing centers, it is even more painful, downright maddening, to read one's own professional obituary; to find, in the pages of a reputable professional journal, that what you do has been judged a failure, written off. Maxine Hairston's "The Winds of Change: Thomas Kuhn and the Revolution in the Teaching of Writing" (*College Composition and Communication*, 33 [1982], 76–88) is an attempt to apply the notion of a "paradigm shift" to the field of composition teaching. In the course of doing so Professor Hairston catalogues, under the subheading "Signs of Change," what she calls "ad hoc" remedies to the writing "crisis":

> Following the pattern that Kuhn describes in his book, our first response to crisis has been to improvise ad hoc measures to try to patch the cracks and keep the system running. Among the first responses were the writing labs that sprang up about ten years ago to give first aid to students who seemed unable to function

within the traditional paradigm. Those labs are still with us, but they're still only
giving first aid and treating symptoms. They have not solved the problem. (p. 82)

What first struck me about this assessment—what probably strikes most people
in the writing center business—is the mistaken history, the notion that writing
labs "sprang up about ten years ago." The fact is, writing "labs," as Professor
Hairston chooses to call them, have been around in one form or another since
at least the 1930s when Carrie Stanley was already working with writers at the
University of Iowa. Moreover, this limited conception of what such places can
do—the fix-it shop image—has been around far longer than ten years, too.
Robert Moore, in a 1950 *College English* article, "The Writing Clinic and the
Writing Laboratory" (7 [1950], 388-393), writes that "writing clinics and
writing laboratories are becoming increasingly popular among American universities and colleges as remedial agencies for removing students' deficiencies
in composition" (p. 388).

Still, you might think that I ought to be happier with Professor Hairston's
position than with, say, Professor Walvoord's. And to some extent I am: even if
she mistakenly assumes that the skill and drill model represents all writing
centers equally well, she at least recognizes its essential futility. Nevertheless—
and this is what bothers me most about her position—her dismissal fails to lay
the blame for these worst versions of writing centers on the right heads. According to her "sprang up" historical sketch, these places simply appeared—like so
many mushrooms?—to do battle with illiteracy. "They" are still with "us," but
"they" haven't solved the problem. What is missing here is a doer, an agent, a
creator—someone to take responsibility. The implication is that "they" done it—
"they" being, apparently, the places themselves.

But that won't wash. "They," to borrow from Walt Kelly, is *us*: members of English departments, teachers of writing. Consider, as evidence, the pattern of writing
center origins as revealed in back issues of *The Writing Lab Newsletter*: the castoff,
windowless classroom (or in some cases, literally, closet), the
battered desks, the old textbooks, a phone (maybe), no budget, and, almost inevitably, a director with limited status—an untenured or non-tenure track faculty member, a teaching assistant, an undergraduate, a "paraprofessional," etc. Now who do
you suppose has determined what is to happen in that center? Not the director,
surely; not the staff, if there is one. The mandate is clearly from the sponsoring
body, usually an English department. And lest you think that things are better where
space and money are not such serious problems, I urge you to visit a center where
a good bit of what is usually grant money has been spent in the first year or two of
the center's operation. Almost always, the money will have been used on materials:
drills, texts, machines, tapes, carrells, headphones—the works. And then the director, hired on "soft" money, without political clout, is locked into an approach because she or he has to justify the expense by using the materials.

Clearly, then, where there is or has been misplaced emphasis on so-called
basics or drill, where centers have been prohibited from dealing with the writing that students do for their classes—where, in short, writing centers have

been of the kind that Professor Hairston is quite correctly prepared to write off—it is because the agency that created the center in the first place, too often an English department, has made it so. The grammar and drill center, the fix-it shop, the first aid station—these are neither the vestiges of some paradigm left behind nor pedagogical aberrations that have been overlooked in the confusion of the "revolution" in the teaching of writing, but that will soon enough be set on the right path, or done away with. They are, instead, the vital and authentic reflection of a way of thinking about writing and the teaching of writing that is alive and well and living in English departments everywhere.

But if my claims are correct—if this is not what writing centers are or, if it is what they are, it is not what they should be—then what are, what *should* they be? What *is* the idea of a writing center? By way of answer, let me return briefly to the family of metaphors by which my sources have characterized their idea of a writing center: Robert Moore's "removing students' deficiencies," Hairston's "first aid" and "treating symptoms," my colleague's "twenty-five errors per page," Hayward's punctuation and grammar referrers, and Walvoord's "carrying the ball for mechanics" (where, at least, writing centers are athletic and not surgical). All these imply essentially the same thing: that writing centers define their province in terms of a given curriculum, taking over those portions of it that "regular" teachers are willing to cede or, presumably, unable to handle. Over the past six years or so I have visited more than fifty centers, and read descriptions of hundreds of others, and I can assure you that there are indeed centers of this kind, centers that can trace their conceptual lineage back at least as far as Moore. But the "new" writing center has a somewhat shorter history. It is the result of a documentable resurgence, a renaissance if you will, that began in the early 1970s. In fact, the flurry of activity that caught Professor Hairston's attention, and which she mistook for the beginnings of the "old" center, marked instead the genesis of a center which defined its province in a radically different way. Though I have some serious reservations about Hairston's use of Kuhn's paradigm model to describe what happens in composition teaching, I will for the moment put things in her terms: the new writing center, far from marking the end of an era, is the embodiment, the epitome, of a new one. It represents the marriage of what are arguably the two most powerful contemporary perspectives on teaching writing: first, that writing is most usefully viewed as a process; and second, that writing curricula need to be student-centered. This new writing center, then, defines its province not in terms of some curriculum, but in terms of the writers it serves.

To say that writing centers are based on a view of writing as a process is, original good intentions notwithstanding, not to say very much anymore. The slogan—and I daresay that is what it has become—has been devalued, losing most of its impact and explanatory power. Let me use it, then, to make the one distinction of which it still seems capable: in a writing center the object is to make sure that writers, and not necessarily their texts, are what get changed by instruction. In axiom form it goes like this: our job is to produce better writers, not better writing. Any given project—a class assignment, a law school application letter, an encyclopedia entry, a dissertation proposal—is for the writer the prime, often the exclusive concern. That particular text, its success or failure, is what brings them to talk to us in the first place. In the center, though, we look beyond or through that particular project, that particular text, and see it as an occasion for addressing *our* primary concern, the process by which it is produced.

At this point, however, the writing-as-a-process slogan tends to lose its usefulness. That "process," after all, has been characterized as everything from the reception of divine inspiration to a set of nearly algorithmic rules for producing the five paragraph theme. In between are the more widely accepted and, for the moment, more respectable descriptions derived from composing aloud protocols, interviews, videotaping, and so on. None of those, in any case, represent the composing process we seek in a writing center. The version we want can only be found, in as yet unarticulated form, in the writer we are working with. I think probably the best way to describe a writing center tutor's relationship to composing is to say that a tutor is a holist devoted to a participant-observer methodology. This may seem, at first glance, too passive—or, perhaps, too glamorous, legitimate, or trendy—a role in which to cast tutors. But consider this passage from Paul Diesing's *Patterns of Discovery in the Social Sciences* (Hawthorne, N.Y.: Aldine, 1971):

> Holism is not, in the participant-observer method, an a priori belief that everything is related to everything else. It is rather the methodological necessity of pushing on to new aspects and new kinds of evidence in order to make sense of what one has already observed and to test the validity of one's interpretations. A belief in the organic unity of living systems may also be present, but this belief by itself would not be sufficient to force a continual expansion of one's observations. It is rather one's inability to develop an intelligible and validated partial model that drives one on. (p. 167)

How does this definition relate to tutors and composing? Think of the writer writing as a kind of host setting. What we want to do in a writing center is fit into—observe and participate in—this ordinarily solo ritual of writing. To do this, we need to do what any participant-observer must do: see what happens during this "ritual," try to make sense of it, observe some more, revise our model, and so on indefinitely, all the time behaving in a way the host finds acceptable. For validation and correction of our model, we quite naturally rely on the writer, who is, in turn, a willing collaborator in—and, usually, beneficiary of—the entire process. This process precludes, obviously, a reliance on or a clinging to any predetermined models of "the" composing process, except as crude topographical guides to what the "territory" of composing processes might look like. The only composing process that matters in a writing center is "a" composing process, and it "belongs" to, is acted out by, only one given writer.

It follows quite naturally, then, that any curriculum—any plan of action the tutor follows—is going to be student-centered in the strictest sense of that term. That is, it will not derive from a generalized model of composing, or be based on where the student ought to be because she is a freshman or sophomore, but will begin from where the student is, and move where the student moves—an approach possible only if, as James Moffett suggests in *Teaching the Universe of Discourse* (Boston: Houghton Mifflin, 1968), the teacher (or tutor in this case) "shifts his gaze from the subject to the learner, for the subject is in the learner" (p. 67). The result is what might be called a pedagogy of direct intervention. Whereas in the "old" center instruction tends to take place after or apart from writing, and tends to focus on the correction of textual problems, in the "new" center the teaching takes place as much as possible during writing, during the activity being learned, and tends to focus on the activity itself.

I do not want to push the participant-observer analogy too far. Tutors are not, finally, researchers: they must measure their success not in terms of the constantly changing model they create, but in terms of changes in the writer. Rather than being fearful of disturbing the "ritual" of composing, they observe it and are charged to change it: to interfere, to get in the way, to participate in ways that will leave the "ritual" itself forever altered. The whole enterprise seems to me most natural. Nearly everyone who writes likes—and needs—to talk about his or her writing, preferably to someone who will really listen, who knows how to listen, and knows how to talk about writing too. Maybe in a perfect world, all writers would have their own ready auditor—a teacher, a classmate, a roommate, an editor—who would not only listen but draw them out, ask them questions they would not think to ask themselves. A writing center is an institutional response to this need. Clearly writing centers can never hope to satisfy this need themselves; on my campus alone, the student-to-tutor ratio would be about a thousand to one. Writing centers are simply one manifestation—polished and highly visible—of a dialogue about writing that is central to higher education.

As is clear from my citations in the first half of this essay, however, what seems perfectly natural to me is not so natural for everyone else. One part of the difficulty, it seems to me now, is not theoretical at all, but practical, a question of coordination or division of labor. It usually comes in the form of a question like this: "If I'm doing process-centered teaching in my class, why do I need a writing center? How can I use it?" For a long time I tried to soft-pedal my answers to this question. For instance, in my dissertation ("Writing Centers: A Sourcebook," Diss. SUNY at Albany, 1978) I talked about complementing or intensifying classroom instruction. Or, again, in our center we tried using, early on, what is a fairly common device among writing centers, a referral form; at one point it even had a sort of diagnostic taxonomy, a checklist, by which teachers could communicate to us their concerns about the writers they sent us.

But I have come with experience to take a harder, less conciliatory position. The answer to the question in all cases is that teachers, as teachers, do not need, and cannot use, a writing center: only writers need it, only writers can use it. You cannot parcel out some portion of a given student for us to deal with ("You take care of editing, I'll deal with invention"). Nor should you require that all of your students drop by with an early draft of a research paper to get a reading from a fresh audience. You should not scrawl, at the bottom of a failing paper, "Go to the Writing Center." Even those of you who, out of genuine concern, bring students to a writing center, almost by the hand, to make sure they know that we won't hurt them—even you are essentially out of line. Occasionally we manage to convert such writers from people who have to see us to people who want to, but most often they either come as if for a kind of detention, or they drift away. (It would be nice if in writing, as in so many things, people would do what we tell them because it's good for them, but they don't. If and when *they* are ready, we will be here.)

In short, we are not here to serve, supplement, back up, complement, reinforce, or otherwise be defined by any external curriculum. We are here to talk to writers. If they happen to come from your classes, you might take it as a compliment to your assignments, in that your writers are engaged in them enough to want to talk about their work. On the other hand, we do a fair amount of trade in people working on ambiguous or poorly designed assignments, and far too much work with writers whose writing has received caustic, hostile, or otherwise unconstructive commentary.

I suppose this declaration of independence sounds more like a declaration of war, and that is obviously not what I intend, especially since the primary casualties would be the students and writers we all aim to serve. And I see no reason that writing centers and classroom teachers cannot cooperate as well as coexist. For example, the first rule in our Writing Center is that we are professionals at what we do. While that does, as I have argued, give us the freedom of self-definition, it also carries with it a responsibility to respect our fellow professionals. Hence we never play student-advocates in teacher-student relationships. The guidelines are very clear. In all instances the student must understand that we support the teacher's position completely. (Or, to put it in less loaded terms—for we are not teacher advocates either—the instructor is simply part of the rhetorical context in which the writer is trying to operate. We cannot change that context: all we can do is help the writer learn how to operate in it and other contexts like it.) In practice, this rule means that we never evaluate or second-guess any teacher's syllabus, assignments, comments, or grades. If students are unclear about any of those, we send them back to the teacher to get clear. Even in those instances I mentioned above—where writers come in confused by what seem to be poorly designed assignments, or crushed by what appear to be unwarrantedly hostile comments—we pass no judgment, at least as far as the student is concerned. We simply try, every way we can, to help the writer make constructive sense of the situation.

In return, of course, we expect equal professional courtesy. We need, first of all, instructors' trust that our work with writers-in-progress on academic assignments is not plagiarism, any more than a conference with the teacher would be—that, to put it the way I most often hear it, we will not write students' papers for them. Second, instructors must grant us the same respect we grant them—that is, they must neither evaluate nor second-guess our work with writers. We are, of course, most willing to talk about that work. But we do not take kindly to the perverse kind of thinking represented in remarks like, "Well, I had a student hand in a paper that he took to the writing center, and it was *still* full of errors." The axiom, if you will recall, is that we aim to make better writers, not necessarily—or immediately—better texts.

Finally, we can always use classroom teachers' cooperation in helping us explain to students what we do. As a first step, of course, I am asking that they revise their thinking about what a writing center can do. Beyond that, in our center we find it best to go directly to the students ourselves. That is, rather than sending out a memo or announcement for the teachers to read in their classes, we simply send our staff, upon invitation, into classes to talk with students or, better yet, to do live tutorials. The standard presentation, a ten-minute affair, gives students a person, a name, and a face to remember the Center by. The live tutorials take longer, but we think they are worth it. We ask the instructor to help us find a writer willing to have a draft (or a set of notes or even just the assignment) reproduced for the whole class. Then the Writing Center person does, with the participation of the entire class, what we do in the Center: talk about writing with the writer. In our experience the instructors learn as much about the Center from these sessions as the students

To argue that writing centers are not here to serve writing class curricula is not to say, however, that they are here to replace them. In our center, anyway, nearly every member of the full-time staff is or has been a classroom teacher of writing. Even our undergraduate tutors work part of their time in an introductory writing course. We all recognize and value the power of classroom teaching, and we take pride in ourselves as professionals in that setting too. But working in both situations makes us acutely aware of crucial differences between talking about writing in the context of a class, and talking about it in the context of the Center. When we hold student conferences in our classes, we are the teacher, in the writers' minds especially, the assigner and evaluator of the writing in question. And for the most part we are pretty busy people, with conference appointments scheduled on the half hour, and a line forming outside the office. For efficiency the papers-in-progress are in some assigned form—an outline, a first draft, a statement of purpose with bibliography and note cards; and while the conference may lead to further composing, there is rarely the time or the atmosphere for composing to happen during the conference itself. Last but not least, the conference is likely to be a command performance, our idea, not the writer's.

When we are writing center tutors all of that changes. First of all, conferences are the writer's idea; he or she seeks us out. While we have an appointment book that offers half hour appointment slots, our typical session is fifty minutes, and we average between three and four per writer; we can afford to give a writer plenty of time. The work-in-progress is in whatever form the writer has managed to put it in, which may make tutoring less efficient, but which clearly makes it more student-centered, allowing us to begin where the writers are, not where we told them to be. This also means that in most cases the writers come prepared, even anxious to get on with their work, to begin or to keep on composing. Whereas going to keep a conference with a teacher is, almost by definition, a kind of goal or deadline—a stopping place—going to talk in the writing center is a means of getting started, or a way to keep going. And finally—in a way subsuming all the rest—we are not the teacher. We did not assign the writing, and we will not grade it. However little that distinction might mean in our behaviors, it seems to mean plenty to the writers.

What these differences boil down to, in general pedagogical terms, are timing and motivation. The fact is, not everyone's interest in writing, their need or desire to write or learn to write, coincides with the fifteen or thirty weeks they spend in writing courses—especially when, as is currently the case at so many institutions, those weeks are required. When writing does become important, a writing center can be there in a way that our regular classes cannot. Charles Cooper, in an unpublished paper called "What College Writers Need to Know" (1979), puts it this way:

> The first thing college writers need to know is that they can improve as writers and the second is that they will never reach a point where they cannot improve further. One writing course, two courses, three courses may not be enough. If they're on a campus which takes writing seriously, they will be able to find the courses they need to feel reasonably confident they can fulfill the requests which will be made of them in their academic work. . . . Throughout their college years they should also be able to find on a drop-in, no-fee basis expert tutorial help with any writing problem they encounter in a paper. (p. 1)

A writing center's advantage in motivation is a function of the same phenomenon. Writers come looking for us because, more often than not, they are genuinely, deeply engaged with their material, anxious to wrestle it into the best form they can: they are motivated to write. If we agree that the biggest obstacle to overcome in teaching anything, writing included, is getting learners to decide that they want to learn, then what a writing center does is cash in on motivation that the writer provides. This teaching at the conjunction of timing and motivation is most strikingly evident when we work with writers doing "real world" tasks: application essays for law, medical, and graduate schools, newspaper and magazine articles, or poems and stories. Law school application writers are suddenly willing—sometimes overwhelmingly so—to concern themselves with audience, purpose, and persona, and to revise over and over again. But we see the same excitement in writers working on literature or history or philosophy papers, or preparing dissertation proposals, or getting ready to tackle comprehensive exams. Their primary concern is with their material, with some existential context where new ideas must merge with old, and suddenly writing is a vehicle, a means to an end, and not an end in itself. These opportunities to talk with excited writers at the height of their engagement with their work are the lifeblood of a writing center.

The essence of the writing center method, then, is this talking. If we conceive of writing as a relatively rhythmic and repeatable kind of behavior, then for a writer to improve that behavior, that rhythm, has to change—preferably, though not necessarily, under the writer's control. Such changes can be fostered, of course, by work outside of the act of composing itself—hence the success of the classical discipline of imitation, or more recent ones like sentence combining or the tagmemic heuristic, all of which, with practice, "merge" with and affect composing. And, indeed, depending on the writer, none of these tactics would be ruled out in a writing center. By and large, however, we find that the best breaker of old rhythms, the best creator of new ones, is our style of live intervention, our talk in all its forms.

The kind of writing does not substantially change the approach. We always want the writer to tell us about the rhetorical context—what the purpose of the writing is, who its audience is, how the writer hopes to present herself. We want to know about other constraints—deadlines, earlier experiences with the same audience or genre, research completed or not completed, and so on. In other ways, though, the variations on the kind of talk are endless. We can question, praise, cajole, criticize, acknowledge, badger, plead—even cry. We can read: silently, aloud, together, separately. We can play with options. We can both write—as, for example, in response to sample essay exam questions—and compare opening strategies. We can poke around in resources—comparing, perhaps, the manuscript conventions of the Modern Language Association with those of the American Psychological Association. We can ask writers to compose aloud while we listen, or we can compose aloud, and the writer can watch and listen.

In this essay, however, I will say no more about the nature of this talk. One reason is that most of what can be said, for the moment, has been said in print already. There is, for example, my own "Training Tutors to Talk About Writing" (*CCC*, 33, [1982] 434-41), or Muriel Harris' "Modeling: A Process Method of Teaching" (*College English*, 45, [1983], 74-84) And there are several other sources, including a couple of essay collections, that provide some insights into the hows and whys of tutorial talk.[2]

A second reason, though, seems to me more substantive, and symptomatic of the kinds of misunderstanding I have tried to dispel here. We don't know very much, in other than a practitioner's anecdotal way, about the dynamics of the tutorial. The same can be said, of course, with regard to talk about writing in any setting—the classroom, the peer group, the workshop, the teacher-student conference, and so on. But while ignorance of the nature of talk in those settings does not threaten their existence, it may do precisely that in writing centers. That is, given the idea of the writing center I have set forth here, talk is everything. If the writing center is ever to prove its worth in other than quantitative terms—numbers of students seen, for example, or hours of tutorials provided—it will have to do so by describing this talk: what characterizes it, what effects it has, how it can be enhanced.

Unfortunately, the same "proofreading-shop-in-the-basement" mentality that undermines the pedagogical efforts of the writing center hampers research as well. So far most of the people hired to run such places have neither the time, the training, nor the status to undertake any serious research. Moreover, the few of us lucky enough to even consider the possibility of research have found that there are other difficulties. One is that writing center work is often not considered fundable—that is, relevant to a wide enough audience—even though there are about a thousand such facilities in the country, a figure which suggests that there must be at least ten to fifteen thousand tutorials every school day, and even though research into any kind of talk about writing is relevant for the widest possible audience. Second, we have discovered that focusing our scholarly efforts on writing centers may be a professional liability. Even if we can publish our work (and that is by no means easy), there is no guarantee that it will be viewed favorably by tenure and promotion review committees. Composition itself is suspect enough; writing centers, a kind of obscure backwater, seem no place for a scholar.

These conditions may be changing. Manuscripts for *The Writing Center Journal*, for example, suggest that writing center folk generally are becoming more research-oriented; there were sessions scheduled at this year's meetings of the MLA and NCTE on research in or relevant to writing centers. In an even more tangible signal of change, the State University of New York has made funds available for our Albany center to develop an appropriate case study methodology for writing center tutorials. Whether this trend continues or not, my point remains the same. Writing centers, like any other portion of a college writing curriculum, need time and space for appropriate research and reflection if they are to more clearly understand what they do, and figure out how to do it better. The great danger is that the very misapprehensions that put them in basements to begin with may conspire to keep them there.

It is possible that I have presented here, at least by implication, too dismal a portrait of the current state of writing centers. One could, as a matter of fact, mount a pretty strong argument that things have never been better. There are, for example, several regional writing center associations that have annual meetings, and the number of such associations increases every year. Both *The Writing Lab Newsletter* and *The Writing Center Journal*, the two publications in the field, have solid circulations. This year at NCTE, for the first time, writing center people met as a recognized National Assembly, a major step up from their previous Special Interest Session status.

And on individual campuses all over the country, writing centers have begun to expand their institutional roles. So, for instance, some centers have established resource libraries for writing teachers. They sponsor readings or reading series by poets and fiction writers, and annual festivals to celebrate writing of all kinds. They serve as clearinghouses for information on where to publish, on writing programs, competitions, scholarships, and so on; and they sponsor such competitions themselves, even putting out their own publications. They design and conduct workshops for groups with special needs—essay exam takers, for example, or job application writers. They are involved with, or have even taken over entirely, the task of training new teaching assistants. They have played central roles in the creation of writing-across-the-curriculum programs. And centers have extended themselves beyond their own institutions, sending tutors to other schools (often high schools), or helping other institutions set up their own facilities. In some cases, they have made themselves available to the wider community, often opening a "Grammar Hotline" or "Grammaphone"—a service so popular at one institution, in fact, that a major publishing company provided funding to keep it open over the summer.

Finally, writing centers have gotten into the business of offering academic credit. As a starting point they have trained their tutors in formal courses or, in some instances, "paid" their tutors in credits rather than money. They have set up independent study arrangements to sponsor both academic and non-academic writing experiences. They have offered credit-bearing courses of their own; in our center, for example, we are piloting an introductory writing course that uses Writing Center staff members as small group leaders.

I would very much like to say that all this activity is a sure sign that the idea of a writing center is here to stay, that the widespread misunderstandings I described in this essay, especially those held so strongly in English departments, are dissolving. But in good conscience I cannot. Consider the activities we are talking about. Some of them, of course, are either completely or mostly public relations: a way of making people aware that a writing center exists, and that (grammar hotlines aside) it deals in more than usage and punctuation. Others—like the resource library, the clearinghouse, or the training of new teaching assistants—are more substantive, and may well belong in a writing center, but most of them end up there in the first place because nobody else wants to do them. As for the credit generating, that is simply pragmatic. The bottom line in academic budget making is calculated in student credit hours; when budgets are tight, as they will be for the foreseeable future, facilities that generate no credits are the first to be cut. Writing centers even really good writing centers—have proved no exception.

None of these efforts to promote writing centers suggest that there is any changed understanding of the idea of a writing center. Indeed it is as though what writing centers do that really matters—talking to writers—were not enough. That being the case, enterprising directors stake out as large a claim as they can in more visible or acceptable territory. All of these efforts—and, I assure you, my center does its share—have about them an air of shrewdness, or desperation, the trace of a survival instinct at work. I am not such a purist as to suggest that these things are all bad. At the very least they can be good for staff morale. Beyond that I think they may eventually help make writing centers the centers of consciousness about writing on campuses, a kind of physical locus for the ideas and ideals of college or university or high school commitment to writing—a status to which they might well aspire and which, judging by results on a few campuses already, they can achieve.

But not this way, not via the back door, not—like some marginal ballplayer—by doing whatever it takes to stay on the team. If writing centers are going to finally be accepted, surely they must be accepted on their own terms, as places whose primary responsibility, whose only reason for being, is to talk to writers. That is their heritage, and it stretches back farther than the late 1960s or the early 1970s, or to Iowa in the 1930s—back, in fact, to Athens, where in a busy marketplace a tutor called Socrates set up the same kind of shop: open to all comers, no fees charged, offering, on whatever subject a visitor might propose, a continuous dialectic that is, finally, its own end.

Notes

[1] "Assessing Attitudes Toward the Writing Center," *The Writing Center Journal*, 3, No. 2 (1983), 1-11.

[2] See, for example, *Tutoring Writing: A Sourcebook for Writing Labs*, ed. Muriel Harris (Glenview, Ill.: Scott-Foresman, 1982); and *New Directions for College Learning Assistance: Improving Writing Skills*, ed. Phyllis Brooks and Thom Hawkins (San Francisco: Jossey-Bass, 1981).

Collaboration, Control, and the Idea of a Writing Center

*Andrea Lunsford*_____
OHIO STATE UNIVERSITY

Andrea Lunsford has helped define for writing instructors the significance of collaborative learning and the social construction of knowledge. In this essay, Lunsford extends her discussion to writing center pedagogy. As she shows us, collaborative writing centers pose "a threat as well as a challenge to the status quo in higher education" by challenging the firmly held notion of authorship as a solitary activity and knowledge as "individually derived, individually held." Lunsford argues that writing centers are excellent sites for undertaking the difficult task of "creating a collaborative environment" that "promotes excellence" and "encourages active learning." Her essay, which originally appeared in 1991 in The Writing Center Journal, *is especially helpful for tutors in providing an overview of social constructionism and its impact on writing center philosophies. In essence, the essay establishes a theoretical context for the work tutors do by contrasting the collaborative writing center with earlier writing center models, shaped by expressivism and current traditional rhetoric.*

THE TRIPLE FOCUS OF MY TITLE reflects some problems I've been concentrating on as I thought about and prepared for the opportunity to speak last week at the Midwest Writing Centers Association meeting in St. Cloud, and here at the Pacific Coast/Inland Northwest Writing Centers meeting in Le Grande. I'll try as I go along to illuminate—or at least to complicate—each of these foci, and I'll conclude by sketching in what I see as a particularly compelling idea of a writing center, one informed by collaboration and, I hope, attuned to diversity.

As some of you may know, I've recently written a book on collaboration, *in* collaboration with my dearest friend and coauthor, Lisa Ede. *Singular Texts/ Plural Authors: Perspectives on Collaborative Writing* was six years in the research and writing, so I would naturally gravitate to principles of collaboration in this or any other address.

Yet it's interesting to me to note that when Lisa and I began our research (see "Why Write . . . Together?"), we didn't even use the term "collaboration"; we identified our subjects as "co- and group-writing." And when we presented our first paper on the subject at the 1985 CCCC meeting, ours was the only such paper at the conference, ours the only presentation with "collaboration" in the title. Now, as you know, the word is everywhere, in every journal, every conference program, on the tip of every scholarly tongue. So—collaboration, yes. But why control? Because as the latest pedagogical bandwagon, collaboration often masquerades as democracy when it in fact practices the same old authoritarian control. It thus stands open to abuse and can, in fact, lead to poor teaching and poor learning. And it can lead—as many of you know—to disastrous results in the writing center. So amidst the rush to embrace collaboration, I see a need for careful interrogation and some caution.

We might begin by asking where the collaboration bandwagon got rolling. Why has it gathered such steam? Because, I believe, collaboration both in theory and practice reflects a broad-based epistemological shift, a shift in the way we view knowledge. The shift involves a move from viewing knowledge and reality as things exterior to or outside of us, as immediately accessible, individually knowable, measurable, and shareable—to viewing knowledge and reality as mediated by or constructed through language in social use, as socially constructed, contextualized, as, in short, the product of *collaboration*.

I'd like to suggest that collaboration as an embodiment of this theory of knowledge poses a distinct threat to one particular idea of a writing center. This idea of a writing center, what I'll call "The Center as Storehouse," holds to the earlier view of knowledge just described—knowledge as exterior to us and as directly accessible. The Center as Storehouse operates as [an] information station or storehouse, prescribing and handing out skills and strategies to individual learners. They often use "modules" or other kinds of individualized learning materials. They tend to view knowledge as individually derived and held, and they are not particularly amenable to collaboration, sometimes actively hostile to it. I visit lots of Storehouse Centers, and in fact I set up such a center myself, shortly after I had finished an M.A. degree and a thesis on William Faulkner.

Since Storehouse Centers do a lot of good work and since I worked very hard to set up one of them, I was loathe to complicate or critique such a center. Even after Lisa and I started studying collaboration in earnest, and in spite of the avalanche of data we gathered in support of the premise that collaboration is the norm in most professions (American Consulting Engineers Council, American Institute of Chemists, American Psychological Institute, Modern Language Association, Professional Services Management Association, International City Management Association, Society for Technical Communication), I was still a very reluctant convert.

Why? Because, I believe, collaboration posed another threat to my way of teaching, a way that informs another idea of a writing center, which I'll call "The Center as Garret." Garret Centers are informed by a deep-seated belief in individual "genius," in the Romantic sense of the term. (I need hardly point out that this belief also informs much of the humanities and, in particular, English studies.) These Centers are also informed by a deep-seated attachment to the American brand of individualism, a term coined by Alexis de Tocqueville as he sought to describe the defining characteristics of this Republic.

Unlike Storehouse Centers, Garret Centers don't view knowledge as exterior, as information to be sought out or passed on mechanically. Rather they see knowledge as interior, as inside the student, and the writing center's job as helping students get in touch with this knowledge, as a way to find their unique voices, their individual and unique powers. This idea has been articulated by many, including Ken Macrorie, Peter Elbow, and Don Murray, and the idea usually gets acted out in Murray-like conferences, those in which the tutor or teacher listens, voices encouragement, and essentially serves as a validation of the students' "I-search." Obviously, collaboration problematizes Garret Centers as well, for they also view knowledge as interiorized, solitary, individually derived, individually held.

As I've indicated, I held on pretty fiercely to this idea as well as to the first one. I was still resistant to collaboration. So I took the natural path for an academic faced with this dilemma: I decided to do more research. I did a *lot* of it. And, to my chagrin, I found more and more evidence to challenge my ideas, to challenge both the idea of Centers as Storehouses or as Garrets. Not incidentally, the data I amassed mirrored what my students had been telling me for years: not the research they carried out, not their dogged writing of essays, not *me* even, but their work in groups, their *collaboration*, was the most important and helpful part of their school experience. Briefly, the data I found all support the following claims:

1. Collaboration aids in problem finding as well as problem solving.
2. Collaboration aids in learning abstractions.
3. Collaboration aids in transfer and assimilation; it fosters interdisciplinary thinking.
4. Collaboration leads not only to sharper, more critical thinking (students must explain, defend, adapt), but to deeper understanding of *others*.
5. Collaboration leads to higher achievement in general. I might mention here the Johnson and Johnson analysis of 122 studies from 1924–1981, which included every North American study that considered achievement or performance data in competitive, cooperative/collaborative, or individualistic classrooms. Some 60% showed that collaboration promoted higher achievement, while only 6% showed the reverse. Among studies comparing the effects of collaboration and independent work, the results are even more strongly in favor of collaboration.

   Moreover, the superiority of collaboration held for all subject areas and all age groups. See "How to Succeed Without Even Vying," *Psychology Today,* September 1986.

6. Collaboration promotes excellence. In this regard, I am fond of quoting Hannah Arendt: "For excellence, the presence of others is always required."

7. Collaboration engages the whole student and encourages active learning; it combines reading, talking, writing, thinking; it provides practice in both synthetic and analytic skills.

Given these research findings, why am I still urging caution in using collaboration as our key term, in using collaboration as the idea of the kind of writing center I now advocate?

First, because creating a collaborative environment and truly collaborative tasks is damnably difficult. Collaborative environments and tasks must *demand* collaboration. Students, tutors, teachers must really need one another to carry out common goals. As an aside, let me note that studies of collaboration in the workplace identify three kinds of tasks that seem to call consistently for collaboration: high-order problem defining and solving; division of labor tasks, in which the job is simply too big for any one person; and division of expertise tasks. Such tasks are often difficult to come by in writing centers, particularly those based on the Storehouse or Garret models.

A collaborative environment must also be one in which goals are clearly defined and in which the jobs at hand engage everyone fairly equally, from the student clients to work-study students to peer tutors and professional staff. In other words, such an environment rejects traditional hierarchies. In addition, the kind of collaborative environment I want to encourage calls for careful and ongoing monitoring and evaluating of the collaboration or group process, again on the part of all involved. In practice, such monitoring calls on each person involved in the collaboration to build a *theory* of collaboration, a theory of group dynamics.

Building such a collaborative environment is also hard because getting groups of any kind going is hard. The students', tutors', and teachers' prior experiences may work against it (they probably held or still hold to Storehouse or Garret ideas); the school day and term work against it; and the drop-in nature of many centers, including my own, works against it. Against these odds, we have to figure out how to constitute groups in our centers; how to allow for evaluation and monitoring; how to teach, model, and learn about careful listening, leadership, goal setting, and negotiation—all of which are necessary to effective collaboration.

We must also recognize that collaboration is hardly a monolith. Instead, it comes in a dizzying variety of modes about which we know almost nothing. In our books, Lisa and I identify and describe two such modes, the hierarchical and the dialogic, both of which our centers need to be well versed at using. But it stands to reason that these two modes perch only at the tip of the collaborative iceberg.

As I argued earlier, I think we must be cautious in rushing to embrace collaboration because collaboration can also be used to reproduce the status quo; the rigid hierarchy of teacher-centered classrooms is replicated in the tutor-centered writing center in which the tutor is still the seat of all authority but is simply pretending it isn't so. Such a pretense of democracy sends badly mixed messages. It can also lead to the kind of homogeneity that squelches diversity, that waters down ideas to the lowest common denominator, that erases rather than values difference. This tendency is particularly troubling given our growing awareness of the roles gender and ethnicity play in all learning. So regression toward the mean is not a goal I seek in an idea of a writing center based on collaboration.

The issue of control surfaces most powerfully in this concern over a collaborative center. In the writing center ideas I put forward earlier, where is that focus of control? In Storehouse Centers, it seems to me control resides in the tutor or center staff, the possessors of information, the currency of the Academy. Garret Centers, on the other hand, seem to invest power and control in the individual student knower, though I would argue that such control is often appropriated by the tutor/teacher, as I have often seen happen during Murray or Elbow style conferences. Any center based on collaboration will need to address the issue of control explicitly, and doing so will not be easy.

It won't be easy because what I think of as successful collaboration (which I'll call Burkean Parlor Centers), collaboration that is attuned to diversity, goes deeply against the grain of education in America. To illustrate, I need offer only a few representative examples:

1. Mina Shaughnessy, welcoming a supervisor to her classroom in which students were busily collaborating, was told, "Oh . . . I'll come back when you're teaching."
2. A prominent and very distinguished feminist scholar has been refused an endowed chair because most of her work had been written collaboratively.
3. A prestigious college poetry prize was withdrawn after the winning poem turned out to be written by three student collaborators.
4. A faculty member working in a writing center was threatened with dismissal for "encouraging" group-produced documents.

I have a number of such examples, all of which suggest that—used unreflectively or uncautiously—collaboration may harm professionally those who seek to use it and may as a result further reify a model of education as the top-down transfer of information (back to The Storehouse) or a private search for Truth (back to The Garret). As I also hope I've suggested, collaboration can easily degenerate into busy work or what Jim Corder calls "fading into the tribe."

So I am very, very serious about the cautions I've been raising, about our need to examine carefully what we mean by collaboration and to explore how those definitions locate control. And yet I still advocate—with growing and deepening conviction—the move to collaboration in both classrooms and centers. In short, I am advocating a third, alternative idea of a writing center, one I know many of you have already brought into being. In spite of the very real risks involved, we need to embrace the idea of writing centers as Burkean Parlors, as centers for collaboration. Only in doing so can we, I believe, enable a student body and citizenry to meet the demands of the twenty-first century. A recent Labor Department report tells us, for instance, that by the mid-1990s workers will need to read at the 11th grade level for even low-paying jobs; that workers will need to be able not so much to solve prepackaged problems but to identify problems amidst a welter of information or data; that they will need to reason from complex symbol systems rather than from simple observations; most of all that they will need to be able to work with others who are different from them and to learn to negotiate power and control (Heath).

The idea of a center I want to advocate speaks directly to these needs, for its theory of knowledge is based not on positivistic principles (that's The Storehouse again), not on Platonic or absolutist ideals (that's The Garret), but on the notion of knowledge as always contextually bound, as always socially constructed. Such a center might well have as its motto Arendt's statement: "For excellence, the presence of others is always required." Such a center would place control, power, and authority not in the tutor or staff, not in the individual student, but in the negotiating group. It would engage students not only in solving problems set by teachers but in identifying problems for themselves; not only in working as a group but in monitoring, evaluating, and building a theory of how groups work; not only in understanding and valuing collaboration but in confronting squarely the issues of control that successful collaboration inevitably raises; not only in reaching consensus but in valuing dissensus and diversity.

The idea of a center informed by a theory of knowledge as socially constructed, of power and control as constantly negotiated and shared, and of collaboration as its first principle presents quite a challenge. It challenges our ways of organizing our centers, of training our staff and tutors, of working with teachers. It even challenges our sense of where we "fit" in this idea. More importantly, however, such a center presents a challenge to the institution of higher education, an institution that insists on rigidly controlled individual performance, on evaluation as punishment, on isolation, on the kinds of values that took that poetry prize away from three young people or that accused Mina Shaughnessy of "not teaching."

This alternative, this third idea of a writing center, poses a threat as well as a challenge to the status quo in higher education. This threat is one powerful and largely invisible reason, I would argue, for the way in which many writing centers have been consistently marginalized, consistently silenced. But organizations like this one are gaining a voice, are finding ways to imagine into being centers as Burkean Parlors for collaboration, writing centers, I believe, which can lead the way in changing the face of higher education.

So, as if you didn't already know it, you're a subversive group, and I'm delighted to have been invited to participate in this collaboration. But I've been talking far too long by myself now, so I'd like to close by giving the floor to two of my student collaborators. The first—like I was—was a reluctant convert to the kind of collaboration I've been describing tonight. But here's what she wrote to me some time ago:

> Dr. Lunsford: I don't know exactly what to say here, but I want to say something. So here goes. When this Writing Center class first began, I didn't know what in the hell you meant by collaboration. I thought—hey! yo!—you're the teacher and you know a lot of stuff. And you better tell it to me. Then I can tell it to the other guys. Now I know that you know even more than I thought. I even found out I know a lot. But that's not important. What's important is knowing that knowing doesn't just happen all by itself, like the cartoons show with a little light bulb going off in a bubble over a character's head. Knowing happens with other people, figuring things out, trying to explain, talking through things. What I know is that we are all making and remaking our knowing and ourselves with each other every day—you just as much as me and the other guys, Dr. Lunsford. We're all—all of us together—collaborative re-creations in process. So—well—just wish me luck.

And here's a note I received just as I got on the plane, from another student/collaborator:

> I had believed that Ohio State had nothing more to offer me in the way of improving my writing. Happily, I was mistaken. I have great expectations for our Writing Center Seminar class. I look forward to every one of our classes and to every session with my 110W students [2 groups of 3 undergraduates he is tutoring]. I sometimes feel that they have more to offer me than I to them. They say the same thing, though, so I guess we're about even, all learning together. (P.S. This class and the Center have made me certain I want to attend graduate school.)

These students embody the kind of center I'm advocating, and I'm honored to join them in conversation about it, conversation we can continue together now.

Works Cited

Corder, Jim W. "Hunting for Ethos Where They Say It Can't Be Found." *Rhetoric Review* 7 (1989): 299–316.

Ede, Lisa S., and Andrea A. Lunsford. "Why Write . . . Together?" *Rhetoric Review* 1 (1983): 150–58.

——. *Singular Texts/Plural Authors: Perspectives on Collaborative Writing.* Carbondale: Southern Illinois UP, 1990.

Heath, Shirley Brice. "The Fourth Vision: Literate Language at Work." *The Right to Literacy.* Ed. Andrea A. Lunsford, Helen Moglen, and James Slevin. New York: Modern Language Association, 1990.

Khon, Alfie. "How to Succeed Without Even Vying." *Psychology Today* Sept. 1986: 22–28.

INTERPERSONAL DYNAMICS

Freud in the Writing Center:
The Psychoanalytics of Tutoring Well

*Christina Murphy*_____

TEXAS CHRISTIAN UNIVERSITY

*Christina Murphy explores the quality and importance of the interpersonal
relationships that tutors build with students by comparing such relationships to
those psychoanalysts develop with their clients. "A good psychoanalyst and a good
tutor both function to awaken individuals to their potentials and to channel their
creative energies toward self-enhancing ends," Murphy writes. To do so, tutors must
form a bond of trust with students, who, in coming to the writing center for help,
"make themselves vulnerable . . . to understanding or misunderstanding, judgment
or acceptance, approval or disapproval." The relationship a student forms with a
tutor differs from those formed with classroom teachers in that it is voluntary, more
personal, and aimed at solving the student's problems. Because of this difference,
the tutor-student bond "often is primarily supportive and affective, secondarily
instructional, and always directed to each student as an individual in a unique,
one-to-one interpersonal relationship." By introducing the psychoanalytic principles
of personal empowerment through interaction, the essay, which originally appeared
in* The Writing Center Journal *in 1989, also offers writing center tutors a theoretical bridge between the expressionist and social constructionist schools of thought.*

"A WRITING TEACHER IS LIKE a Psychoanalyst, Only Less Well Paid," Jay Parini
declares in a recent essay in *The Chronicle of Higher Education.* One part of
Parini's equation is almost self-evident to writing teachers since they know
that, of the degreed professionals, college professors are among the least
well paid for their efforts. The second half of the equation, the ways in
which teaching writing mirrors aspects of the psychoanalytic process, is
perhaps less apparent and clear. I would like to suggest that this correlation
is most apparent in the interaction between tutors in a writing center and
those students who come to seek their services. Unlike students who enroll
in courses for a spectrum of reasons from "the course is required" to "it fits
into my schedule," students come to a writing center for one reason only—
they want help with their writing.

The fact that students come to the writing center wanting help and
assuming they will receive it places those students in a different type of
relationship with the tutor than with the instructor in a traditional classroom setting. While the teacher's role is primarily informative and focused
upon the method of presentation that will best convey instruction to the
class as a whole, the tutor's role often is primarily supportive and affective,

43

secondarily instructional, and always directed to each student as an individual in a unique, one-to-one interpersonal relationship.

As in psychoanalysis, the quality of that interpersonal relationship between therapist and client, tutor and student, determines how successful the interaction as a whole will be. L. D. Goodstein, in an essay titled "What Makes Behavior Change Possible," argues that the quality of a therapeutic relationship is "an essential ingredient of behavior change." And what are the qualities of a good relationship of supportive intervention like therapy or tutoring? Carl Rogers states that all good therapists or supportive interveners manifest a real concern for those in their charge. They direct to these individuals, in Roger's terms, "unconditional positive regard" by demonstrating a basic interest, concern, and desire to help another human being. Empathetic understanding expressed as honesty or a genuine openness of character is the second quality. The more this quality is perceived or felt by clients or students, the more impact it has on them.

Rogers places such a high premium upon the nature of the interpersonal relationship between therapist and client because so many of the people who enter in therapy are "hurt"—they are suffering from negative feelings or emotions, interpersonal problems, and inadequate and unsatisfying behaviors. The same is often true of individuals who come to a writing center. They, too, are "hurt" in that they display insecurities about their abilities as writers or even as academic learners, express fear to the tutor that they will be treated in the same judgmental or abusive way that they have been treated by teachers or fellow students before, or exhibit behavior patterns of anxiety, self-doubt, negative cognition, and procrastination that only intensify an already difficult situation.

> "I know you're going to tear this paper to shreds," they say, "but here goes anyway."
> "I've never been able to write. This is hopeless."
> "I know you can't help me, but I thought I'd try the writing center anyway."
> Or maybe they are defensive: "This teacher gives dumb assignments. If he'd just give me something I could write about, I know I'd do better."
> Sometimes they are self-deceived: "I've always made A's in English in high school, so I know I should be making A's in college, too."
> Other times they are self-defeating: "Can you help me with this paper? It's due at 2:00."
> "Well, that only gives us thirty minutes."
> "I know, but maybe you could go over it and help me write an ending."

By and large, the students who come "hurt" to a writing center are those who suffer from writer's block or a high degree of inhibiting anxiety associated with the process of producing writing that will be evaluated by others. These students demonstrate the principle endorsed by Rogers and other humanistic educators that learning is not simply a cognitive process. These students do not have difficulty writing because of any inherent flaws or limitations in the type of instruction they have received from their teachers or because they necessarily lack abilities as writers. Instead, they represent individuals whose talents as writers and as academic learners can be realized only within a specific set of conditions and circumstances. C. H. Patterson, in *Theories of Counseling and Psychotherapy*, indicates that, for these types of individuals with inherent abilities but inhibiting fears, the psychoanalytic concept of information theory may provide the most productive conceptual understanding and approach. This theory "views the individual as actively attending to, selecting, operating on, organizing, and transforming the information provided by the environment and by internal sources. Thus, the individual defines stimuli and events and constructs his or her own world" (668).

For the tutor, "information-processing psychology is concerned with understanding the nature of internal events, and more particularly, processes occurring within the individual as he or she handles and organizes his or her experience" (Wexler and Rice 15–20). Achieving the goals and possibilities of this theory, or of any client-centered theory, requires an empathetic bond between tutor and student in the interventive process. When such a structure is established by the tutor, the relationship that develops is experienced by the student as "safe, secure, free from threat, and supporting but not supportive" (Patterson 498). Rogers describes this process as "one dealing with warm living people who are dealt with by warm living counselors" (Patterson 499).

Some might argue against or minimize the importance of the relationship that develops between tutor and student or claim that, even though this relationship is potent in itself, it really bears little resemblance to the relationships established in a psychoanalytic setting. Truax and Carkhuff, in *Toward Effective Counseling and Psychotherapy*, would contend, however, that fundamental and profound similarities exist amongst all the interventive processes, from therapy, to education, to the managerial interactions of employer and employee. They state "the person (whether a counselor, therapist, or teacher) who is better able to communicate warmth, genuineness, and accurate empathy is more effective in interpersonal relationships no matter what the goal of the interaction" (116–17).

Most of what goes on in a writing center is talking and the range of interpersonal interactions available through words. In coming to a writing center for assistance, students must explain to a tutor what they want and what they hope to achieve. In the course of this type of interaction, the students make themselves vulnerable in opening themselves up to understanding or misunderstanding, judgment or acceptance, approval or disapproval.

Jim W. Corder, in an interesting essay titled "A New Introduction to Psychoanalysis, Taken as a Version of Modern Rhetoric," describes psychoanalysis, from a rhetorical perspective, as "the talking cure." Thomas Szasz calls psychotherapy "iatrology," or "healing words" (29). Psychotherapy, like rhetoric, understands the power of words, especially "healing words." As psychotherapists or tutors, we function like the old medicine man in *Ceremony*, the novel by Leslie Silko, who says, "That was the responsibility that went with being human . . . the story behind each word must be told so that there could be no mistake in the meaning of what had been said" (35). As psychotherapists or tutors, we share with those in our charge the responsibility that goes with being human. And in our very human roles, we share the powers of language to express emotions, to inspire creative thought, and to change perceptions of the self and others. We share the power of language to transform thought and being.

It is to psychotherapy that we owe the clearest model of the types of transformative interactions and outcomes that can occur in a writing center setting. For psychotherapy to be successful, (1) two persons are in contact; (2) one person, the client, generally is in a state of incongruence, being vulnerable or anxious; (3) the other person, the therapist, is congruent in the relationship; (4) the therapist experiences unconditional positive regard toward the client; (5) the therapist experiences an empathetic understanding of the client's internal frame of reference; and (6) the client perceives, at least to a minimal degree, the therapist's empathetic understanding of the client's internal frame of reference. As a result of the process of psychotherapy, (1) the client is more congruent, more open to his or her experiences, less defensive; (2) as a result, the client is more realistic, objective, extensional in his or her perceptions; (3) the client is consequently more effective in problem-solving; (4) as a result of the increased congruence of self and experience, his or her vulnerability to threat is reduced; (5) as a result of the lowering of his or her vulnerability to threat or defeat, the client has an increased degree of self-regard; and (6) as a result of all of the above factors, the client's behavior is more creative, more uniquely adaptive and more fully expressive of his or her own values (Patterson 486–87).

If we substitute *tutor* and *student* here for *therapist* and *client*, the model holds true for the learning strategies and experiential awarenesses that go on in a writing center environment. A good psychoanalyst and a good tutor both function to awaken individuals to their potentials and to channel their creative energies toward self-enhancing ends. Within the focus of the one-on-one tutorial, the student and tutor work to interpret the cognitive strategies the student has employed to be expressive, insightful, concise, and clear. To work with the student in deciphering and assessing creative processes, in suggesting new ways to interpret data, methods of inquiry, and philosophical perspectives, and in determining a philosophy of personal expression requires from the tutor a sensitivity to the affective and intellectual dimensions of the student's personality. At the core of tutoring and psychotherapy are the interactional dynamics of a search for insight that involves an intimate transference of trust and vulnerability between two individuals intent upon and intimately involved in finding answers.

Jim W. Corder states that "human frailty sets immediate and overpowering limits":

> Every utterance belongs to, exists in, issues from, and reveals a rhetorical universe. Every utterance comes from somewhere (its inventive origin), emerges as a structure, and manifests itself as a style. All of the features of utterance—inven-

tion, structure, and style—cycle, reciprocate, and occur simultaneously. Each of us is a gathering place for a host of rhetorical universes. Some of them we share with others, indeed with whole cultures; some of them we inhabit alone, and some of them we occupy without knowing that we do. Each of us is a busy corner where multiple rhetorical universes intersect. (141)

Part of the transformative power of a writing center is that it is a setting in which rhetorical universes are shared. In this way, the tutoring process, like the psychotherapeutic process, partakes in the power of language to reshape and empower consciousness. James Hillman in *Re-Visioning Psychology* calls words "independent carriers of soul between people" (9). Perhaps no better description of the interaction that goes on in tutoring and in therapy can be found. If it is true that words transform consciousness, and changes in consciousness transform the self, then language-based processes like therapy and tutoring provide a dynamic for self-awareness and self-actualization. To this extent, they are liberatory philosophies in the manner that Paolo Freire uses that term to describe how the power of words can empower the consciousnesses of ourselves and others.

Perhaps, when all is said and done, the old medicine man of Leslie Silko's *Ceremony* is a Freudian, believing in the humanness of liberation and in the power of reintegrating consciousness through the language of one's tribe. Perhaps the old medicine man works daily in writing centers across America, responding to the questions of those who come, apprentice fashion, to learn.

"Can you help me with my writing?"
"Yes, I can, but first let us start with your words."

Works Cited

Corder, Jim W. "A New Introduction to Psychoanalysis, Taken as a Version of Modern Rhetoric." *Pre/Text* 5.3–4 (1984): 137–69.

Goodstein, L. D. "What Makes Behavior Change Possible?" *Contemporary Psychology* 22 (1977): 578–79.

Hillman, James. *Re-Visioning Psychology.* New York: Harper and Row, 1975.

Parini, Jay. "A Writing Teacher is Like a Psychoanalyst, Only Less Well Paid." *The Chronicle of Higher Education* 2 Nov. 1988. B2.

Patterson, C. H. *Theories of Counseling and Psychotherapy.* 3rd ed. New York: Harper and Row, 1980.

Rogers, Carl R. "The Necessary and Sufficient Conditions of Therapeutic Personality Change." *Journal of Consulting Psychology* 21 (1957): 95–103.

Schor, Ira, and Paolo Freire. *A Pedagogy for Liberation: Dialogues on Transforming Education.* South Hadley: Bergin and Garvey, 1987.

Silko, Leslie Marmon. *Ceremony.* New York: Viking Penguin, 1977.

Szasz, Thomas. *The Myth of Psychotherapy: Mental Healing as Religion, Rhetoric, and Repression.* New York: Anchor Press/Doubleday, 1978.

Truax, C. B., and R. R. Carkhuff. *Toward Effective Training in Counseling and Psychotherapy.* Chicago: Aldine, 1967.

Wexler, D. A., and L. N. Rice, eds. *Innovations in Client-Centered Therapy.* New York: Wiley, 1984.

Humor and the Serious Tutor

Steve Sherwood _____

TEXAS CHRISTIAN UNIVERSITY

Laughter and the humor that inspires it have a place in writing centers, Steve Sherwood suggests. A bit of well-aimed humor may energize a bored student or help another break through writer's block. Used judiciously, humor can build tutor-student rapport, calm students' fears, soften criticism, and even enhance creativity by generating unexpected connections between ideas. Indeed, in the best instances, "the intelligent and humane use of humor" can help tutors create a setting in which productive collaboration can thrive. Sherwood's essay is valuable in indicating the relationship of humor to creative thinking and to higher-level cognitive skills, and in suggesting ways that tutors can use humor to engage students actively in the tutoring process. This essay first appeared in The Writing Center Journal *in 1993.*

RECENT SCHOLARSHIP WRESTLES with the issue of creating a setting within writing centers that encourages genuine collaboration between those who seek advice (or input) and those who give it. Some scholarship suggests that too often the people who fund, administer, and use writing centers see the facilities as primarily remedial. Among other problems, this attitude promotes the "us-and-them mentality" that Richard Leahy cautions against (45). Lex Runciman, too, blames misconceptions about the meaning of *tutor* and *tutoring* for assumptions made by students, administrators, and tutors themselves that "writing centers serve only bad writers" ("Defining" 28) and are little more than emergency rooms for critically ill grammar. Both scholars urge us to create an environment "in which everyone is free to develop his or her own best writing processes" (Leahy 45), where good writers go "in order to make enlightened decisions about context, organization, idea development, tone, and the like" (Runciman, "Defining" 33). To create such a place, Leahy urges us to "foster a community of people who love writing and like to share their writing with each other" (45). As a logical first step, Runciman suggests we abandon terms that carry remedial connotations (e.g., *tutor* and *tutoring*) and adopt terms that more accurately describe who we are and what we do. Although I agree that we need to encourage an enlightened, collaborative environment in writing centers, I believe we can achieve this goal (whether or not we rename ourselves and our work) through the intelligent and humane use of humor.

At first glance, laughter and the humor that inspires it may seem incompatible with the mission of the writing center. Helping people improve their writing is serious business, after all, and tutors who resort to humor risk much. Our attempts at wit, however well-intended, may fall flat or backfire resulting in confused, wounded, impatient, or angry student writers. Likewise, our colleagues may see us as lightweights who approach the job frivolously. They may be right, especially about those who misuse humor by ridiculing students to make themselves feel superior. But a writing center without laughter can be a grim, fearful place, and we must not disregard the role humor can play in facilitating interactive learning. John Morreall says,

All the features of humor . . . especially its connection with imagination and creativity, and the flexibility of perspective which it brings, are valuable not just in aesthetic education but in all education. Unfortunately, however, many teachers see no place for humor in education. (*Taking* 97)

Those willing to use this tutoring tool must do so cautiously, of course, putting the student's best interest before their own egos. Still they will find that humor can build a bridge between tutor and student, can distance students from their fears, soften any necessary criticism, and, as Morreall suggests, plant the seeds of flexibility and creativity which may, in some cases, free students to do their best work. In doing so, humor may also help us create in the writing center the kind of setting Leahy and Runciman call for in which collaboration can thrive.

Objections to humor in any academic setting, including the writing center, usually begin with the age-old perception that humor is essentially derisive. In other words, those in superior positions (i.e., tutors) laugh at the infirmities of those in inferior positions (i.e., students). As Plato says, "[P]owerless ignorance may be considered ridiculous" (Morreall, *Philosophy* 12) making it a proper target of derision. Schopenhauer adds, "the laughter of others at what we do or say seriously offends us" because the "laugh of scorn announces . . . how incongruous were the conceptions [we] cherished with the reality which is now revealing itself" (61).

Students often bring to us their most cherished (or sometimes their most despised) conceptions—their writing projects. Part of our job is to reveal what we perceive of reality, as it applies to their writing, without doing undue harm to their egos. It's hard to conceive of a greater disaster for a writing center than for its tutors, from a position of superiority (real or imagined), to ridicule writers' weaknesses (real or imagined). As peer tutor coordinator for Texas Christian University's writing center, I was appalled one day to see a tutor do this very thing. The tutor would read a passage from the student's paper, then chuckle and say, "I'm sorry, but this doesn't make any sense at all. What do you mean here?" The student's reaction, a blend of humiliation and rage, should have told the tutor his approach wasn't working. Instead, the student soon ended the session, and to my knowledge never returned to the center.

If an incident like this fails to alert us to the dangers of mixing humor and tutoring, we can easily find other reasons to beware. This is especially true for those among us who subscribe to a "hierarchical model of education, a model which places a knowledgeable teacher [or tutor] on a higher level than ignorant students" (Runciman, "Defining" 29). In Umberto Eco's *The Name of the Rose*, an old monk (appropriately blind) censures his brothers for laughing at humorous illustrations, saying, "Our Lord did not have to employ such foolish things to point out the straight and narrow path to us" (81). To hide the only copy of Aristotle's "lost" treatise on humor, fearing its discovery might legitimize humor as a scholastic subject, the old monk resorts to murder. Normally, our own colleagues will not act so drastically to maintain the sober atmosphere of the writing center. But like Eco's monk, some of them may view laughter as a fruitless, even dangerous, detour on the straight and narrow path to knowledge. Many academics "project a one-dimensional attitude which tells students that education, and life in general, is serious business . . . a series of lessons to be remembered and problems to be solved" (Morreall, *Taking* 98). Laughter undermines these goals, momentarily freeing those who laugh from the rules of proper conduct, even from rational thought (103). To authority figures (including some tutors), this temporary loss of control may be reason enough to fear laughter. More dangerous still is the chance that a student may briefly gain superiority by deriding a tutor's own cherished conceptions, especially since we all tend to "laugh more heartily when the victim is a person of dignity, that is, a person to whom we normally feel inferior" (Monro 103). Maybe we can understand then, why, faced with these concerns, an authoritative tutor may avoid humor or use it as a tool of repression with the "unavowed intention to humiliate, and consequently to correct" students (Boskin 255).

For writing teachers, especially those of us who teach one-on-one in writing centers, dominating students through humor, or any other means, runs counter to our mission. As benevolent advisors we seek to dominate (if anything) only a student's writing problems. We're far more interested—or at least we should be—in cultivating skills or talent, and we can do this only with a student's help. To get that help, we seek to develop with the student a relationship of respect, trust, even friendship. So we feel dismayed at a tutor's clumsy or cruel use of humor when a relationship might have been built rather than a bridge burnt.

This isn't to say that in the interest of cementing relationships a tutor should begin every session, Jay Leno style, with an opening monologue. Some students are all business: grim, determined, and impatient with anything that resembles frivolity. And that's fine. But even in dealing with such students, we can maintain a humorous perspective that may rub off, without further antagonizing them, and help build the rapport necessary for successful collaboration. As Morreall says, "To laugh with another person for whatever reason, even if only at a piece of absurdity, is to get closer to that person" (*Taking* 115).

McCluskey and Walker write about classroom teachers in *The Doubtful Gift*, but their advice on relating to gifted children applies nearly as well to the tutor-student relationship. The gifted, they say, are

> quick to appreciate the humorous aspects of a situation, to play on words, or to enjoy a clever joke or pun . . . The teacher needs to be able to join in and laugh with the kids (and at herself upon occasion). If a teacher is lacking this ingredient, she might do well to go to some pains to try to develop a sense of humour—with the gifted, she will need it! (81-82)

Experience tells us that not every student who comes to a writing center for advice is gifted. The average tutor probably falls a bit short of the genius level, too. But if humor can ease relations with gifted students (predisposed to laughter) we ought to find it at least as helpful in easing relations with ordinary students (young or old), especially those who see us as adversaries. Recently, for example, a student began a tutorial by saying, "I hate this paper, I hate to write, and I hate my professor. I only came here because she made me."

"Wow!" I said, mostly to avoid reflecting his hostility. "That's a lot to deal with in one session. If we work hard, maybe we can help you overcome your feelings about the paper. But it could take weeks before you learn to enjoy writing, and for all I know, you may always hate your professor."

He responded with a harsh snort. "So you think you're going to teach me to like writing?"

"Not today," I reminded him (or ever, as it turned out). But by sharing a laugh, brief and bitter though it was, we moved far enough past his initial resentment to work together. And as he left, he conceded he no longer hated his paper; he merely detested it.

As it so often does, fear probably lay at the heart of his anger; fortunately, the laughter that builds a bridge can also calm fears. When they write, students face a daunting array of threats to their self-esteem from such external forces as deadlines, grades, parental (or spousal) expectations, and tough professors, and from such internal forces as unrealistic goals, fear of failure, and what psychiatrists term "social fears." Among the latter, Stewart Agras lists fear of criticism, fear of disapproval, fear of rejection, fear of meeting a stranger, and fear of authority figures (122), all of which students may confront at writing centers.

Clearly laughter can soothe these social fears. "When we are anxious about meeting someone," Morreall says, ". . . the first laugh we share (if it occurs) will be important, for it will mark the other person's acceptance of us" (*Taking* 115–16). Among other advantages, shared laughter usually occurs between people who, if only for a short time, find themselves relating as equals. Morreall suggests that humor has a more profound effect on fear by distancing us from our troubles (*Taking* 104) thus helping us rise above situations in which failure seems likely. William H. Martineau might as well be making a direct reference to fearful student writers when he says, "For the oppressed, [humor] operates to bolster morale and hope; the humor becomes a compensatory device, making the fear and tragedy of the moment seem perhaps only temporary" (104).

As tutors, we can help students make use of this compensatory device. Consider Christie, for instance, who came to see me at the writing center one day and said, in deadly earnest, "I have to get an 'A' on this paper."

I nodded warily. "That's what everyone hopes for."

"You don't understand," she said. "Mom's been grooming me for medical school since before I was born, but I have a 'C' in lit. If I don't get an 'A' on this paper, there's no way I'll get a 'B' in the class, which means I won't get into the pre-med program, which means I'll never be a doctor, which means my mom will kill me."

I smiled, and she looked outraged. "I'm serious!" she insisted. But when the absurdity of her own reasoning hit home, she laughed, which effectively shifted her focus from the terrifying prospect of failure to the more immediate task of improving her paper. As it turned out, this was a blessing because the paper's many logical fallacies made it an unlikely candidate for the "A" that would save Christie's life—unless she put aside her fears and got back to work.

At this crucial stage of the tutoring process, we may find a humorous outlook particularly useful. For once we've bridged the initial social barriers and temporarily calmed the students' fears, we must—whether acting as authority figures or collaborators—give a candid opinion of the strengths and weaknesses of their work. Most of us have felt the sting of brutal criticism. If we're honest, we'll admit we didn't much like the experience even if (or *especially* if) the critics were right, and, in hindsight, we see how much they helped us. In telling a student our version of the truth, we must make sure it hurts as little as possible. Occasionally weighing the stark truth against the fragile ego can be tricky.

Humor provides a point of balance. Hard lessons go down more easily and more palatably with a dose of it. In fact, Monro calls humor "the sugar round the pill" (169), and both Martineau (117) and Morreall (*Taking* 116) recognize its value as a method of subtly criticizing faults while leaving a person's ego intact. My own writing teacher, William Allen, softened the truth about my first novel by reading the worst passages aloud in a slow Texas drawl. I nearly suffocated, laughing out of the kind of embarrassment that hurts the soul as much as the belly. He made his point, though, in a way that left me bruised but unbroken and without jeopardizing our relationship.

Allen's comical reading of my work looks uncannily like my peer tutor's derision of a student's phrases. There are differences, though. I was in my late twenties and emotionally equipped to bounce back. And instead of laughing scornfully *at* me, Allen soon had me laughing at myself, giving me the necessary distance from my gaffes to deal with them constructively. In fact, he resisted laughing at all, except in sympathetic reaction to my laughter, and seemed to sense just how far to push before easing up.

Before applying this technique to the writing center, we must learn to gauge how each individual will respond and act accordingly. Reading a student to choose the right approach is a fine skill—one that my peer tutor lacked. Although a bit of well-aimed humor may energize bored students, others might be too touchy or downtrodden to tolerate humor directed at their writing. In these cases, we're better off dispensing with humor or limiting ourselves to self-deprecation, recalling times when the challenges our students are facing baffled us. Once, a distraught student complained that when she read her essay aloud in class, the other students laughed in all the wrong places. I told her about the time I tried to sell a humor piece to a prestigious New York magazine whose editor actually took the trouble to jot a rejection note that said, "This is weird. And it isn't nearly as funny as you seem to think it is."

"Ouch! So what did you do?"

"A few months later, when I understood what he meant, I rewrote the piece and sold it to another magazine whose editor said it was the funniest he'd read all year."

"So you think I should rewrite my paper?" she asked.

"Only if you think there's a chance the class was right," I said.

Approached with care most students, even the grimly serious or downtrodden, can benefit from and appreciate humor-based tutoring. One student wrote in a graduate school application, for example, that her interest in psychology stemmed from childhood when her brother suffered from severe separation anxiety. "As I'm sure you understand," she concluded, "I'm anxious to start a career in my chosen field of child psychology."

"Good essay," I said, then pointed to the last line, "but are you sure you want to say *anxious* here?"

"What should I say? *Extremely anxious?*"

"No," I said and smiled cautiously. "Considering your chosen field that might be an unfortunate choice of words."

She stared at me for a while, then looked appalled.

"I'd say *eager*," I suggested.

"Oh, I will," she said with an embarrassed laugh. "My God, and with my brother suffering from separation anxiety. What would they think?"

As helpful as humor can be in overcoming fears and softening criticism, perhaps it plays its most vital role in liberating creative potential. Research shows a clear relationship between humor and creativity (Greenlaw and McIntosh 135). Indeed, Claudia Cornett believes humor "stimulates the kinds of thinking processes used frequently by highly creative people," and engaging in it "can free up or increase the amount and quality of a person's creative capacities" (11). The mind responds this way because, as L. W. Kline says, humor "not only creates [a] sense of freedom but also assures us that we may temporarily escape from the uniformities and mechanism of life" (qtd. in Monro 178). All of this makes humor especially useful in fostering collaboration. One afternoon, for instance, frustrated in the search for just the right term to use in a key sentence—a synonym for *unalterable*—a student and I began substituting words that were progressively more inappropriate until we were laughing out loud. By turning his diction upside down and introducing nonsense into the somber, straightforward world of his essay, the student eventually decided the tone and structure of his paper were as rigid as his language. He later opted for a softer, more flexible tone that opened the way for fresh ideas.

The connection of humor to creative thinking starts with the simple notion of freedom, but it runs deeper. Monro says a joke often depends on "the linking of disparates: the importing into one sphere of ideas which belong in another" (238). Greenlaw and McIntosh advise teachers who wish to enhance creative thinking in students to, among other things, encourage a tolerance for ambiguity, paradox, and analogy, all of which are in some way based upon forging connections between apparently unconnected elements (220). The random give and take of a truly collaborative tutorial often generates unexpected links between ideas (Arnold Schwarzenegger as radical feminist, for instance) that can strike students as absurd and, therefore, funny. This process of making connections, Monro says, "is in itself a good formula for humour" (238).

Known as synthesis, it's a fair formula for writing—and for creativity in general. Einstein once said that "combinatory play" with diverse mental elements "seems to be the essential feature of productive thought" (qtd. in Simonton 179). Walter Nash, as well, contends that the human virtue of creativeness "lies in perceiving relationships, making connections, designing an order, projecting a shape" (217). He adds that "as long as we present arguments, tell stories, write poems, make jokes . . . we shall be practising [sic] nothing other than a form of rhetoric" (217–18).

In writing centers, where we often see individuals only once, we may find it difficult to assess the ultimate impact of a humorous approach to tutoring. I *can* recall students who, having seen an idea in a new, humorous light, left the center ready to attempt a revision. One of them, Zoe, arrived already punchy from an assignment to analyze the sexual imagery of Whitman's "I Saw in Louisiana a Live-Oak Growing." At one point, with a despairing laugh, she offhandedly joked about the metaphoric possibilities of Whitman's leaf-sprouting twig. Then, as if struck by a revelation, she muttered thanks and rushed off to finish the paper.

I may never know if Zoe's inspiration bore fruit, but I take comfort from an essay by Runciman, titled "Fun?". In it, Runciman argues that a little fun goes a long way toward motivating writers. He cites a student, who, reflecting on his semester's work, says, "I see a growing acceptance of the freedom to write as I please, which is allowing me to almost enjoy writing (I can't believe it)" (160). Unfortunately, neither can many tutors, perhaps because, as Runciman laments,

> One trouble with pleasure (even that resulting from a demanding and rigorous mental activity) is that it's squishy, it's difficult to predict, and talking about it seems vaguely unprofessional. It seems frivolous. (159)

In reality, the pleasure a tutor inspires through humor is anything but unprofessional or frivolous. It can build rapport, calm fears, sweeten criticism, and enhance creativity. Beyond the chance that an occasional one-liner may misfire, the risks of resorting to humor lie chiefly in treating those who come to writing centers not as supplicants for wisdom handed down from on high, but as free individuals, creative and unpredictable, who, in arriving at their own ideas, may challenge our most cherished conceptions. In the process, by encouraging this messy give and take between tutors (or whatever we choose to call them) and students, humor can help transform the tutorial into something that approaches true collaboration.

Works Cited

Agras, Stewart. *Panic: Facing Fears, Phobias, and Anxiety.* New York: Freeman, 1985.

Boskin, Joseph. "The Complicity of Humor: The Life and Death of Sambo." *The Philosophy of Laughter and Humor.* Ed. John Morreall. Albany: State U of New York P, 1987. 250–63.

Cornett, Claudia E. *Learning Through Laughter: Humor in the Classroom.* Bloomington: Phi Delta Kappa, 1986.

Eco, Umberto. *The Name of the Rose.* Trans. William Weaver. New York: Harcourt, 1983. Trans. of *Il Nome Della Rosa,* 1980.

Greenlaw, M. Jean, and Margaret E. McIntosh. *Educating the Gifted: A Sourcebook.* Chicago: American Library Association, 1988.

Leahy, Richard. "Of Writing Centers, Centeredness, and Centrism." *The Writing Center Journal* 13.1 (1992): 43–52.

Martineau, William H. "A Model of the Social Functions of Humor." *The Psychology of Humor: Theoretical Perspectives and Empirical Issues.* Ed. Jeffery H. Goldstein and Paul E. McGhee. New York: Academic P, 1972. 101–24.

McCluskey, Ken W., and Keith D. Walker. *The Doubtful Gift: Strategies for Educating Gifted Children in the Regular Classroom.* Kingston: Frye, 1986.

Monro, D. H. *Argument of Laughter.* Notre Dame: U of Notre Dame P, 1963.

Morreall, John, ed. *The Philosophy of Laughter and Humor.* Albany: State U of New York P, 1987.

———. *Taking Laughter Seriously.* Albany: State U of New York P, 1983.

Nash, Walter. *Rhetoric: The Wit of Persuasion.* Cambridge: Blackwell, 1989.

Runciman, Lex. "Defining Ourselves: Do We Really Want to Use the Word Tutor?" *The Writing Center Journal* 11.1 (1990): 27–33.

———. "Fun?" *College English* 53 (1991): 156–62.

Simonton, Dean K. "Chance Configuration Theory of Scientific Creativity." *Psychology of Science: Contributions to Metascience.* Ed. Barry Gholson et al. Cambridge: Cambridge UP, 1989. 170–213.

"Whispers of Coming and Going": Lessons from Fannie

Anne DiPardo
THE UNIVERSITY OF IOWA

DiPardo's essay, a case study of her work with Fannie, a Native American student, was chosen the outstanding work of scholarship for 1993 by the National Writing Centers Association. DiPardo profiles Fannie's development over a number of writing center tutorials. Through details about Fannie's past and dialogue between Fannie and DiPardo, the reader comes to know Fannie well enough to care about her. The essay also explores the corresponding development of Morgan, a peer tutor, as she struggles with the collaborative techniques she attempts to incorporate in her work with Fannie. DiPardo's essay emphasizes multicultural sensitivity by encouraging tutors to question the assumptions they make about students and to seek clues to the "hidden corners" of a student's past, personality, and methods of learning. DiPardo supports the notion of reflective practice in tutoring by encouraging tutors to be "perennially inquisitive and self-critical" while learning from the students they attempt to teach. Perhaps the essay's greatest value is the insight it offers into an individual student and tutor as they negotiate a relationship. This essay first appeared in The Writing Center Journal *in 1992.*

As a man with cut hair, he did not identify the rhythm of three strands, the whispers of coming and going, of twisting and tying and blending, of catching and of letting go, of braiding.
—Michael Dorris, *A Yellow Raft in Blue Water*

We all negotiate among multiple identities, moving between public and private selves, living in a present shadowed by the past, encountering periods in which time and circumstance converge to realign or even restructure our images of who we are. As increasing numbers of non-Anglo students pass through the doors of our writing centers, such knowledge of our own shape-shifting can help us begin—if *only* begin—to understand the social and linguistic challenges which inform their struggles with writing. When moved to talk about the complexities of their new situation, they so often describe a more radically chameleonic process, of living in non-contiguous worlds, of navigating between competing identities, competing loyalties. "It's like I have two cultures in me," one such student remarked to me recently, "but I can't choose." Choice becomes a moot point as boundaries blur, as formerly distinct selves become organically enmeshed, indistinguishable threads in a dynamic whole (Bakhtin 275; Cintron 24; Fischer 196).

Often placed on the front lines of efforts to provide respectful, insightful attention to these students' diverse struggles with academic discourse, writing tutors likewise occupy multiple roles, remaining learners even while emerging as teachers, perennially searching for a suitable social stance (Hawkins)—a stance existing somewhere along a continuum of detached toughness and warm empathy, and, which like all things ideal, can only be approximated, never definitively located. Even the strictly linguistic dimension of their task is rendered problematic by the continuing paucity of research on the writing of non-mainstream students (see Valdés; "Identifying Priorities"; "Language Issues")—a knowledge gap which likewise complicates our own efforts to provide effective tutor training and support. Over a decade has passed since Mina Shaughnessy eloquently advised basic writing teachers to become students of their students, to consider what Glynda Hull and Mike Rose ("Rethinking," "Wooden Shack") have more recently called the "logic and history" of literacy events that seem at first glance inscrutable and strange. In this age of burgeoning diversity, we're still trying to meet that challenge, still struggling to encourage our tutors to appreciate its rich contours, to discover its hidden rigors, to wrestle with its endless vicissitudes.

This story is drawn from a semester-long study of a basic writing tutorial program at a west-coast university—a study which attempted to locate these tutor-led small groups within the larger contexts of a writing program and campus struggling to meet the instructional needs of non-Anglo students (see DiPardo, "Passport"). It is about one tutor and one student, both ethnic minorities at this overwhelmingly white, middle-class campus, both caught up in elusive dreams and uncertain beginnings. I tell their story not because it is either unusual or typical, but because it seems so richly revealing of the larger themes I noted again and again during my months of data collection—as unresolved tensions tugged continually at a fabric of institutional good intentions, and as tutors and students struggled, with ostensible good will and inexorable frustration, to make vital connections. I tell this story because I believe it has implications for all of us trying to be worthy students of our students, to make sense of our own responses to diversity, and to offer effective support to beginning educators entrusted to our mentorship.

"It, Like, Ruins Your Mind": Fannie's Educational History

Fannie was Navajo, and her dream was to one day teach in the reservation boarding schools she'd once so despised, to offer some of the intellectual, emotional, and linguistic support so sorely lacking in her own educational history. As a kindergartner, she had been sent to a school so far from her home that she could only visit family on weekends. Navajo was the only language spoken in her house, but at school all the teachers were Anglo, and only English was allowed. Fannie recalled that students had been punished for speaking their native language—adding with a wry smile that they'd spoken Navajo anyway, when the teachers weren't around. The elementary school curriculum had emphasized domestic skills—cooking, sewing, and, especially, personal hygiene. "Boarding school taught me to be a housemaid," Fannie observed in one of her essays, "I was hardly taught how to read and write." All her literacy instruction had been in English, and she'd never become literate in Navajo. Raised in a culture that valued peer collaboration (cf. Philips 391–93), Fannie had long ago grasped that Anglo classrooms were places where teachers assume center stage, where students are expected to perform individually: "No," her grade-school teachers had said when Fannie turned to classmates for help, "I want to hear *only* from *you*."

Estranged from her family and deeply unhappy, during fifth grade Fannie had stayed for a time with an aunt and attended a nearby public school. The experience there was much better, she recalled, but there soon followed a series of personal and educational disruptions as she moved among various relatives' homes and repeatedly switched schools. By the time she began high school, Fannie was wondering if the many friends and family members who'd dropped out had perhaps made the wiser choice. By her sophomore year, her grades had sunk "from A's and B's to D's and F's," and she was "hanging out with the wrong crowd." By mid-year, the school wrote her parents a letter indicating that she had stopped coming to class. When her family drove up to get her, it was generally assumed that Fannie's educational career was over.

Against all odds, Fannie finished high school after all. At her maternal grandmother's insistence, arrangements were made for Fannie to live with an aunt who had moved to a faraway west-coast town where the educational system was said to be much stronger. Her aunt's community was almost entirely Anglo, however, and Fannie was initially self-conscious about her English: "I had an accent really bad," she recalled, "I just couldn't communicate." But gradually, although homesick and sorely underprepared, she found that she was holding her own. Eventually, lured by the efforts of affirmative action recruiters, she took the unexpected step of enrolling in the nearby university. "I never thought I would ever graduate from high school," Fannie wrote in one of her essays, adding proudly that "I'm now on my second semester in college as a freshman." Her grandmother had died before witnessing either event, but Fannie spoke often of how pleased she would have been.[1]

Fannie was one of a handful of Native Americans on the campus, and the only Navajo. As a second-semester first-year student, she was still struggling to find her way both academically and socially, still working to overcome the scars of her troubled educational history. As she explained after listening to an audiotape of a tutorial session, chief among these was a lingering reluctance to speak up in English, particularly in group settings:

> *Fannie:* When, when, I'm talking. . . . I'm shy. Because I always think I
> always say something not right, with my English, you know,
> (Pauses, then speaks very softly.) It's hard, though. Like with
> my friends, I do that too. Because I'll be quiet—they'll say,
> "Fannie, you're quiet." Or if I meet someone, I, I don't do it, let
> them do it, I let that person do the talking.
> *A. D.:* Do you wish you were more talkative?
> *Fannie:* I wish! Well I am, when I go home. But when I come here, you
> know, I always think, English is my second language and I
> don't know that much, you know.
> *A. D.:* So back home you're not a shy person?
> *Fannie:* (laughing uproariously) No! (continues laughing).

I had a chance to glimpse Fannie's more audacious side later that semester, when she served as a campus tour guide to a group of students visiting from a distant Navajo high school. She was uncharacteristically feisty and vocal that week, a change strikingly evident on the tutorial audiotapes. Indeed, when I played back one of that week's sessions in a final interview, Fannie didn't recognize her own voice: "Who's that talking?" she asked at first. But even as she recalled her temporary elation, she described as well her gradual sense of loss:

> Sometimes I just feel so happy when someone's here, you know, I feel happy? I
> just get that way. And then (pauses, begins to speak very softly), and then it just
> wears off. And then they're leaving—I think, oh, they're leaving, you know.

While Fannie described their week together as "a great experience," she was disturbed to find that even among themselves, the Navajo students were speaking English: "That bothered me a lot," she admitted, surmising that "they're like embarrassed . . . to speak Navajo, because back home, speaking Navajo fluently all the time, that's like lower class." "If you don't know the language," Fannie wrote in one of her essays, "then you don't know who you are. . . . It's your identity . . . the language is very important." In striking contrast to these students who refused to learn the tribal language, Fannie's grandparents had never learned to speak English: "They were really into their culture, and tradition, and all of that," she explained, "but now we're not that way anymore, hardly, and it's like we're losing it, you know." Fannie hoped to attend a program at Navajo Community College where she could learn to read and write her native language, knowledge she could then pass on to her own students.

Fannie pointed to the high drop-out rate among young Navajos as the primary reason for her people's poverty, and spoke often of the need to encourage students to finish high school and go on to college. And yet, worried as she was about the growing loss of native language and tradition, Fannie also expressed concerns about the Anglicizing effects of schooling. Education is essential, she explained, but young Navajos must also understand its dangers:

> I mean like, sometimes if you get really educated, we don't really want that. Because then, it like ruins your mind, and you use it, to like betray your people, too . . . That's what's happening a lot now.

By her own example, Fannie hoped to one day show her students that it is possible to be both bilingual and bicultural, that one can benefit from exposure to mainstream ways without surrendering one's own identity:

> If you know the white culture over here, and then you know your own culture, you can make a good living with that . . . when I go home, you know, I know Navajo, and I know English too. They say you can get a good job with that

Back home, Fannie's extended family was watching her progress with warm pride, happily anticipating the day when she would return to the reservation to teach. When Fannie went back for a visit over spring break, she was surprised to find that they'd already built her a house: "They sure give me a lot of attention, that's for sure," she remarked with a smile. Many hadn't seen Fannie for some time, and they were struck by the change:

> Everybody still, kind of picture me, still, um, the girl from the past. The one who quit school—and they didn't think of me going to college at all. And they were surprised, they were really surprised. And they were like proud of me too . . . 'cause none of their family is going to college.

One delighted aunt, however, was the mother of a son who was also attending a west-coast college:

> She says, "I'm so happy! I can't wait to tell him, that you're going to college too! You stick in there, Fannie, now don't goof!" I'm like, "I'll try not to!"

"I Always Write Bad Essays": Fannie's Struggles With Writing

On the first day of class, Fannie's basic writing teacher handed out a questionnaire that probed students' perceptions of their strengths and weaknesses as writers. In response to the question, "What do you think is good about your writing?" Fannie wrote, "I still don't know what is good about my writing"; in response to "What do you think is bad about your writing?" she responded, "Everything."

Fannie acknowledged that her early literacy education had been neither respectful of her heritage nor sensitive to the kinds of challenges she would face in the educational mainstream. She explained in an interview that her first instruction in essay writing had come at the eleventh hour, during her senior year of high school: "I never got the technique, I guess, of writing good essays," she explained, "I always write bad essays." While she named her "sentence structure, grammar, and punctuation" as significant weaknesses, she also added that "I have a lot to say, but I can't put it on paper . . . it's like I can't find the vocabulary." Fannie described this enduring block in an in-class essay she wrote during the first week of class:

> From my experience in writing essays were not the greatest. There were times my mind would be blank on thinking what I should write about.
>
> In high school, I learned how to write an essay during my senior year. I learned a lot from my teacher but there was still something missing about my essays. I knew I was still having problems with my essay organization.
>
> Now, I'm attending a university and having the same problems in writing essays. The university put me in basic writing, which is for students who did not pass the placement test. Of course, I did not pass it. Taking basic writing has helped me a lot on writing essays. There were times I had problems on what to write about.
>
> There was one essay I had problems in writing because I could not express my feelings on a paper. My topic was on Mixed Emotions. I knew how I felt in my mind but I could not find the words or expressing my emotions.
>
> Writing essays from my mind on to the paper is difficult for me. From this experience, I need to learn to write what I think on to a paper and expand my essays.

"Yes," her instructor wrote at the bottom of the page, "even within this essay—which is good—you need to provide specific detail, not just general statements." But what did Fannie's teacher find "good" about this essay—or was this opening praise only intended to soften the criticism that followed? Fannie had noted in an interview that she panicked when asked to produce something within 45 minutes: "I just write anything," she'd observed, "but your mind goes blank, too." Still, while this assignment may not have been the most appropriate way to assess the ability of a student like Fannie, both she and her instructor felt it reflected her essential weakness—that is, an inability to develop her ideas in adequate detail.

At the end of the semester, her basic writing teacher confided that Fannie had just barely passed the course, and would no doubt face a considerable struggle in first-year composition. Although Fannie also worried about the next semester's challenge, she felt that her basic writing course had provided valuable opportunities. "I improved a lot," she said in a final interview, "I think I did—I know I did. 'Cause now I can know what I'm trying to say, and in an afternoon, get down to that topic." One of her later essays, entitled "Home," bears witness to Fannie's assertion:

> The day is starting out a good day. The air smells fresh as if it just rained. The sky is full with clouds, forming to rain. From the triangle mountain, the land has such a great view. Below I see hills overlapping and I see six houses few feet from each other. One of them I live in. I can also see other houses miles apart.

> It is so peaceful and beautiful. I can hear birds perching and dogs barking echos from long distance. I can not tell from which direction. Towards north I see eight horses grazing and towards east I hear sheep crying for their young ones. There are so many things going on at the same time.

> It is beginning to get dark and breezy. It is about to rain. Small drops of rain are falling. It feels good, relieving the heat. The rain is increasing and thundering at the same time. Now I am soaked, I have the chills. The clouds is moving on and clearing the sky. It is close to late afternoon. The sun is shining and drying me off. The view of the land is more beautiful and looks greener. Like a refreshment.

> Across from the mountain I am sitting is a mountain but then a plateau that stretches with no ending. From the side looks like a mountain but it is a long plateau. There are stores and more houses on top of the plateau.

> My clothes are now dry and it is getting late. I hear my sister and my brother calling me that dinner is ready. It was a beautiful day. I miss home.

"Good description," her instructor wrote on this essay, "I can really 'see' this scene." But meanwhile, she remained concerned about Fannie's lack of sophistication: "Try to use longer, more complex sentences," she added, "avoid short, choppy ones." Overwhelmed by the demands of composing and lacking strategies for working on this perceived weakness, Fannie took little away from such feedback aside from the impression that her writing remained inadequate.

Although Fannie was making important strides, she needed lots of patient, insightful support if she were to overcome her lack of experience with writing and formidable block. Only beginning to feel a bit more confident in writing about personal experience, she anticipated a struggle with the expository assignments that awaited her:

> She's having us write from our experience. It'll be different if it's like in English 101, you know how the teacher tells you to write like this and that, and I find that one very hard, cause I see my other friends' papers and it's hard. I don't know if I can handle that class.

Fannie was trying to forge a sense of connection to class assignments—she wrote, for instance, about her Native American heritage, her dream of becoming a teacher, and about how her cultural background had shaped her concern for the environment. But meanwhile, as her instructor assessed Fannie's progress in an end-of-term evaluation, the focus returned to lingering weaknesses: "needs to expand ideas w/examples/description/explanation," the comments read, not specifying how or why or to whom. Somehow, Fannie had to fill in the gaps in her teacher's advice—and for the more individualized support she so sorely needed, she looked to the tutorials.

"Are You Learnin' Anything From Me?": The Tutorials

Morgan, Fannie's African American tutor, would soon be student teaching in a local high school, and she approached her work with basic writers as a trial run, a valuable opportunity to practice the various instructional strategies she'd heard about in workshops and seminars. Having grown up in the predominantly Anglo, middle-class community that surrounded the campus, Morgan met the criticisms of more politically involved ethnic students with dogged insistence: "I'm first and foremost a member of the *human* race," she often said, going on to describe her firm determination to work with students of all ethnicities, to help them see that success in the mainstream need not be regarded as cultural betrayal. During the term that I followed her—her second semester of tutoring and the first time she'd worked with non-Anglo students—this enthusiasm would be sorely tested, this ambition tempered by encounters with unforseen obstacles.

Morgan's work with Fannie was a case in point. Although she had initially welcomed the challenge of drawing Fannie out, of helping this shy young woman overcome her apparent lack of self-confidence, by semester's end Morgan's initial compassion had been nearly overwhelmed by a sense of frustration. In an end-of-term interview, she confessed that one impression remained uppermost: "I just remember her sitting there," Morgan recalled, "and talking to her, and it's like, 'well I don't know, I don't know'. . . Fannie just has so many doubts, and she's such a hesitant person, she's so withdrawn, and mellow, and quiet . . . . A lot of times, she'd just say, 'well I don't know what I'm supposed to write . . . . Well I don't like this, I don't like my writing.'"

Although Fannie seldom had much to say, her words were often rich in untapped meaning. Early in the term, for instance, when Morgan asked why she was in college, Fannie searched unsuccessfully for words that would convey her strong but somewhat conflicted feelings:

Fannie: Well . . . (long pause) . . . it's hard . . .

Morgan: You wanna teach like, preschool? Well, as a person who wants to teach, what do you want outta your students?

Fannie: To get around in America you have to have education . . . (unclear).

Morgan: And what about if a student chose not to be educated—would that be ok?

Fannie: If that's what he wants . . .

At this point Morgan gave up and turned to the next student, missing the vital subtext—how Fannie's goal of becoming a teacher was enmeshed in her strong sense of connection to her people, how her belief that one needs an education "to get around" in the mainstream was tempered by insight into why some choose a different path. To understand Fannie's stance towards schooling, Morgan needed to grasp that she felt both this commitment *and* this ambivalence; but as was so often the case, Fannie's meager hints went unheeded.

A few weeks into the semester, Morgan labored one morning to move Fannie past her apparent block on a descriptive essay. Fannie said only that she was going to try to describe her grandmother, and Morgan began by asking a series of questions—about her grandmother's voice, her presence, her laugh, whatever came to Fannie's mind. Her questions greeted by long silences, Morgan admitted her gathering frustration: "Are you learnin' anything from me?" she asked. Morgan's voice sounded cordial and even a bit playful, but she was clearly concerned that Fannie didn't seem to be meeting her halfway. In the weeks that followed, Morgan would repeatedly adjust her approach, continually searching for a way to break through, "to spark something," as she often put it.

The first change—to a tougher, more demanding stance—was clearly signalled as the group brainstormed ideas for their next essays. Instead of waiting for Fannie to jump into the discussion, Morgan called upon her: "Ok, your turn in the hot seat," she announced. When Fannie noted that her essay would be about her home in Arizona, Morgan demanded to know "why it would be of possible interest to us." The ensuing exchange shed little light on the subject:

Fannie: Because it's my home!
Morgan: That's not good enough . . . that's telling me nothing.
Fannie: I was raised there.
Morgan: What's so special about it?
Fannie: (exasperated sigh) I don't know what's so special about it . . .
Morgan: So why do you want to write about it, then?

Morgan's final question still unanswered, she eventually gave up and moved to another student. Again, a wealth of valuable information remained tacit; Morgan wouldn't learn for several weeks that Fannie had grown up on a reservation, and she'd understood nothing at all about her profound bond with this other world.

Two months into the semester, Morgan had an opportunity to attend the Conference on College Composition and Communication (CCCC), and it was there that some of her early training crystallized into a more definite plan of action, her early doubts subsumed by a new sense of authoritative expertise. Morgan thought a great deal about her work with Fannie as she attended numerous sessions on peer tutoring and a half-day workshop on collaborative learning. She returned to campus infused with a clear sense of direction: the solution, Morgan had concluded, was to assume an even more low-profile approach, speaking only to ask open-ended questions or to paraphrase Fannie's statements, steadfastly avoiding the temptation to fill silences with her own ideas and asides. As she anticipated her next encounter with Fannie, she couldn't wait to try out this more emphatic version of what had been called—in conference sessions and her earlier training—a "collaborative" or "non-directive" stance.

Still struggling to produce an already past-due essay on "values," Fannie arrived at their first post-CCCC tutorial hour with only preliminary ideas, and nothing in writing. Remembering the advice of Conference participants, Morgan began by trying to nudge her towards a focus, repeatedly denying that she knew more than Fannie about how to approach the piece:

Morgan: What would you say your basic theme is? And sometimes if you keep that in mind, then you can always, you know, keep that as a focus for what you're writing. And the reason I say that is 'cause when you say, "well living happily wasn't. . . . "

Fannie: (pause) . . . Well, America was a beautiful country, well, but it isn't beautiful anymore.

Morgan: Um hm. Not as beautiful.

Fannie: So I should just say, America was a beautiful country?

Morgan: Yeah. But I dunno—what do you think your overall theme is, that you're saying?

Fannie: (long pause). . . . I'm really, I'm just talking about America.

Morgan: America? So America as . . . ?

Fannie: (pause) . . . Um . . . (pause)

Morgan: Land of free, uh, land of natural resources? As, um, a place where there's a conflict, I mean, there, if you can narrow that, "America." What is it specifically, and think about what you've written, in the rest. Know what I mean?

Fannie: (pause) . . . The riches of America, or the country? I don't know . . .

Morgan: I think you do. I'm not saying there's any right answer, but I, I'm—for me, the reason I'm saying this, is I see this emerging as, you know, (pause) where you're really having a hard time with dealing with the exploitation that you see, of America, you know, you think that. And you're using two groups to really illustrate, specifically, how two different attitudes toward, um the richness and beauty of America, two different, um, ways people have to approach this land. Does that, does this make any sense? Or am I just putting words in your mouth? I don't want to do that. I mean that's what I see emerge in your paper. But I could be way off base.

Fannie: I think I know what you're trying to say. And I can kind of relate it at times to what I'm trying to say.

Morgan: You know, I mean, this is like the theme I'm picking up . . . (pause) I think you know, you've got some real, you know, environmental issues here. I think you're a closet environmentalist here. Which are real true, know what I mean. (pause) And when you talk about pollution, and waste, and, um, those types of things. So I mean, if you're looking at a theme of your paper, what could you pick out, of something of your underlying theme.

Fannie: (pause) . . . The resources, I guess?

Morgan: Well I mean, I don't want you to say, I want you to say, don't say "I guess," is that what you're talkin' about?

Fannie: Yeah.

Morgan: "Yeah?" I mean, it's your paper.

Fannie: I know, I want to talk about the land . . .

Morgan: Ok. So you want to talk about the land, and the beauty of the land . . .

Fannie: Um hm.

Morgan: . . . and then, um, and then also your topic for your, um, to spark your paper . . . what values, and morals, right? That's where you based off to write about America, and the land, you know. Maybe you can write some of these things down, as we're talking, as focussing things, you know. So you want to talk about the land, and then it's like, what do you want to say about the land?

What *did* Fannie "want to say about the land"? Whatever it was, one begins to wonder if it was perhaps lost in her tutor's inadvertent appropriation of these meanings—this despite Morgan's ostensible effort to simply elicit and reflect Fannie's thoughts. While Fannie may well have been struggling to articulate meanings which eluded clear expression in English, as Morgan worked to move her towards greater specificity, it became apparent that she was assuming the paper would express commonplace environmental concerns:

Fannie: I'll say, the country was, um, (pause), more like, I can't say perfect, I mean was, the tree was green, you know, I mean, um, it was clean. (long pause) I can't find the words for it.

Morgan: In a natural state? Um, un-, polluted, um, untouched, um, let me think, tryin' to get a . . .

Fannie: I mean everybody, I mean the Indians too, they didn't wear that (pointing to Morgan's clothes), they only wore buffalo clothing, you know for clothing, they didn't wear like . . . these, you know, cotton, and all that, they were so . . .

Morgan: Naturalistic.

Fannie: Yeah. "Naturalistic," I don't know if I'm gonna use that word . . . I wanna say, I wanna give a picture of the way the land was, before, you know what I'm, what I'm tryin' to say?

The Navajos' connection to the land is legendary—a spiritual nexus, many would maintain, that goes far beyond mainstream notions of what it means to be concerned about the environment. However, later in this session, Morgan observed that Fannie was writing about concerns that worry lots of people— citing recent publicity about the greenhouse effect, the hole in the ozone layer, and the growing interest in recycling. She then brought the session to a close by paraphrasing what she saw as the meat of the discussion and asking, "Is that something that you were tryin' to say, too?" Fannie replied, "Probably. I mean, I can't find the words for it, but you're finding the words for me." Morgan's rejoinder had been, "I'm just sparkin', I'm just sparkin' what you already have there, what you're sayin'. I mean I'm tryin' to tell you what I hear you sayin'."

Morgan laughed as, in an end-of-term interview, she listened again to Fannie's final comment: "I didn't *want* to find the words for her," she mused; "I wanted to show her how she could find 'em for herself." Still, she admitted, the directive impulse had been hard to resist: "I wanted to just give her ideas," Morgan observed, adding that although Fannie had some good things to say, "I wanted her to be able to articulate her ideas on a little higher level." Although it was obvious to Morgan that the ideas in Fannie's paper were of "deep-seated emotional concern," she also saw her as stuck in arid generalities: "'I don't know, it's just such a beautiful country,'" Morgan echoed as she reviewed the audiotape. While Morgan emphasized that she "didn't wanna write the paper for her," she allowed that "it's difficult—it's really hard to want to take the bull by the horns and say, 'don't you see it this way?'" On the one hand, Morgan noted that she'd often asked Fannie what she was getting out of a session, "'cause sometimes I'll think I'm getting through and I'm explaining something really good, and then they won't catch it"; on the other hand, Morgan emphasized again and again that she didn't want to "give away" her own thoughts.

Although Morgan often did an almost heroic job of waiting out Fannie's lingering silences and deflecting appeals to her authority, she never really surrendered control; somehow, the message always came across that Morgan knew more than Fannie about the ideas at hand, and that if she would, she could simply turn over pre-packaged understandings. While her frustration was certainly understandable, I often had the sense that Morgan was insufficiently curious about Fannie's thoughts—insufficiently curious about how Fannie's understandings might have differed from her own, about how they had been shaped by Fannie's background and cultural orientation, or about what she stood to learn from them.

When asked about Fannie's block, a weary Morgan wrote if off to her cultural background:

> You know, I would have to say it's cultural; I'd have to say it's her you know, Native American background and growing up on a reservation . . . maybe . . . she's more sensitive to male-female roles, and the female role being quiet.

On a number of occasions Morgan had speculated that Navajo women are taught to be subservient, a perception that contrasted rather strikingly with Fannie's assertion that she wasn't at all shy or quiet back home.[2] Hoping to challenge Morgan's accustomed view of Fannie as bashful and retiring, in a final interview I played back one of their sessions from the week that a group of Navajo students were visiting the campus. Fannie was uncharacteristically vocal and even aggressive that morning, talking in a loud voice, repeatedly seizing and holding the floor:

> *Fannie:* You know what my essay's on? Different environments. Um, I'm talking, I'm not gonna talk about my relationship between

my brothers, it's so boring, so I'm just gonna talk about both being raised, like my youngest brother being raised on the reservation, and the other being raised over here, and they both have very different, um, um, (Morgan starts to say something, but Fannie cuts her off and continues) characteristics or somethin' like that. You know, like their personalities, you know.

Morgan: Um. That's good. (Morgan starts to say something more, but Fannie keeps going.)

Fannie: It's funny, I'm cutting, I was totally mean to my brother here. (Morgan laughs.) Because, I called, I said that he's a wimp, you know, and my brother, my little brother's being raised on the reservation, is like, is like taught to be a man, he's brave and all that.

Luis: (a student in the group) That's being a man?!

Fannie: And . . .

Luis: That's not being a man, I don't find.

Fannie: (her voice raised) I'm sorry—but that's how I wrote, Ok?! That's your opinion, I mean, and it's . . .

Luis: I think a man is sensitive, caring, and lov—

Fannie: (cutting him off) No, no . . .

Luis: . . . and able to express his feelings. I don't think that if you can go kill someone, that makes you a man.

Fannie: I mean . .

Luis: That's just my opinion (gets up and walks away for a moment).

Fannie: (watching Luis wander off) Dickhead.

Morgan listened with a widening smile to the rest of this session, obviously pleased with Fannie's sometimes combative manner and unflagging insistence that attention be directed back to her. "Ha! Fannie's *so* much more forceful," Morgan exclaimed, "and just more in control of what she wants, and what she needs." When asked what she thought might have accounted for this temporary change, Morgan sidestepped the influence of the visiting students:

> I would love to think I made her feel safe that way. And that I really um, showed her that she had, you know, by my interactions with her, that she really had every right to be strong-willed and forceful and have her opinions and you know, say what she felt that she needed to say, and that she didn't have to be quiet, you know. People always tell me that I influence people that way. You know? (laughs). "You've been hangin' around with Morgan too much!"

Hungry for feedback that she'd influenced Fannie in a positive way, Morgan grasped this possible evidence with obvious pleasure. Fannie was not a student who offered many positive signals, and it was perhaps essential to Morgan's professional self-esteem that she find them wherever she could. In this credit-taking there was, however, a larger irony: if only she'd been encouraged to push a little farther in her own thinking, perhaps she would have found herself assisting more often in such moments of blossoming.

Conclusion: Students as Teachers, Teachers as Students

When Morgan returned from the CCCC with a vision of "collaboration" that cast it as a set of techniques rather than a new way to think about teaching and learning, the insights of panelists and workshop leaders devolved into a fossilized creed, a shield against more fundamental concerns. Morgan had somehow missed the importance of continually adjusting her approach in the light of the understandings students make available, of allowing their feedback to shape her reflections upon her own role. At semester's end, she still didn't know that Fannie was a non-native speaker of English; she didn't know the dimensions of Fannie's inexperience with academic writing, nor did she know the reasons behind Fannie's formidable block.

Even as Morgan labored to promote "collaborative" moments—making an ostensible effort to "talk less," to "sit back more," to enact an instructional mode that would seem more culturally appropriate—Fannie remembered a lifetime of classroom misadventure, and hung back, reluctant. Morgan needed to know something about this history, but she also needed to understand that much else was fluid and alive, that a revised sense of self was emerging from the dynamic interaction of Fannie's past and present. Emboldened by a few treasured days in the company of fellow Navajos, Fannie had momentarily stepped into a new stance, one that departed markedly from her accustomed behavior on reservation and campus alike; but if her confidence recalled an earlier self, her playful combativeness was, as Fannie observed in listening to the tape, a new and still-strange manifestation of something also oddly familiar, something left over from long ago.

Rather than frequent urgings to "talk less," perhaps what Morgan most needed was advice to *listen more*—for the clues students like Fannie would provide, for those moments when she might best shed her teacherly persona and become once again a learner. More than specific instructional strategies, Morgan needed the conceptual grounding that would allow her to understand that authentically collaborative learning is predicated upon fine-grained insight into individual students—of the nature of their Vygotskian "zones of proximal development," and, by association, of the sorts of instructional "scaffolding" most appropriate to their changing needs (Bruner; Langer and Applebee). So, too, did Morgan need to be encouraged toward the yet-elusive understanding that such learning is never unilateral, inevitably entailing a reciprocal influence, reciprocal advances in understanding (Dyson). As she struggled to come to terms with her own ethnic ambivalence, to defend herself against a vociferous chorus proclaiming her "not black enough," Morgan had reason to take heart in Fannie's dramatic and rather trying process of transition. Had she thought to ask, Morgan would no doubt have been fascinated by Fannie's descriptions of this other cultural and linguistic context, with its very different perspectives on education in particular and the world in general (John; Locust). Most of all, perhaps, she would have been interested to know that Fannie was learning to inhabit both arenas, and in so doing, enacting a negotiation of admirable complexity—a negotiation different in degree, perhaps, but certainly not in kind, from Morgan's own.

Having tutored only one semester previously, Morgan was understandably eager to abandon her lingering doubts about her effectiveness, eager for a surefooted sense that she was providing something worthwhile. Her idealism and good intentions were everywhere apparent—in her lengthy meditations on her work, in her eager enthusiasm at the CCCC, in her persistent efforts to try out new approaches, and in the reassurance she extended to me when I confessed that I'd be writing some fairly negative things about her vexed attempts to reach Fannie. Morgan had been offered relatively little by way of preparation and support: beyond a sprinkling of workshops and an occasional alliance with more experienced tutors, she was left largely on her own—alone with the substantial challenges and opportunities that students like Fannie presented, alone to deal with her frustration and occasional feelings of failure as best she could. Like all beginning educators, Morgan needed abundant support, instruction, and modeling if she were to learn to reflect critically upon her work, to question her assumptions about students like Fannie, to allow herself, even at this fledgling stage in her career, to become a reflective and therefore vulnerable practitioner. That is not to suggest that Morgan should have pried into hidden corners of Fannie's past, insisting that she reveal information about her background before she felt ready to do so; only that Morgan be respectfully curious, ever attentive to whatever clues Fannie might have been willing to offer, ever poised to revise old understandings in the light of fresh evidence.

Those of us who work with linguistic minority students—and that's fast becoming us all—must appreciate the evolving dimensions of our task, realizing that we have to reach further than ever if we're to do our jobs well. Regardless of our crowded schedules and shrinking budgets, we must also think realistically about the sorts of guidance new tutors and teachers need if they are to confront these rigors effectively, guiding them towards practical strategies informed by understandings from theory and research, and offering compelling reminders of the need to monitor one's ethnocentric biases and faulty assumptions. Most of all, we must serve as models of reflective practice—perennially inquisitive and self-critical, even as we find occasion both to bless and curse the discovery that becoming students of students means becoming students of ourselves as well.

Notes

[1]"Fannie" was the actual name of this student's maternal grandmother. We decided to use it as her pseudonym to honor this lasting influence.

[2]Morgan's assumption is also contradicted by published accounts of life among the Navajo, which from early on have emphasized the prestige and power of female members of the tribe. Gladys Reichard, an anthropologist who lived among the Navajos in the 1920s, reported that "the Navajo woman enjoys great economic and social prestige as the head of the house and clan and as the manager of economic affairs, and she is not

excluded from religious ritual or from attaining political honors" (55). Navajo women often own substantial property, and children retain the surname of the matrilineal clan; the status accorded women is further reflected in the depictions of female deities in Navajo myths (Terrell 57; 255).

Acknowledgments

Special thanks to Sarah Warshauer Freedman for encouragement and sage advice throughout this project. Thanks also to Don McQuade, Guadalupe Valdés, and the members of my fall 1991 writing research class at The University of Iowa.

This work was supported by a grant from the NCTE Research Foundation.

Works Cited

Applebee, Arthur, and Judith Langer. "Reading and Writing Instruction: Toward a Theory of Teaching and Learning." *Review of Research in Education*. Vol. 13. Ed. E. Z. Rothkopf. Washington, DC: American Educational Research Association, 1986.

Bakhtin, Mikhail Mikhailovich. *The Dialogic Imagination: Four Essays by M. M. Bakhtin*. Ed. Michael Holquist, trans. Caryl Emerson and Michael Holquist. Austin: U of Texas P, 1981.

Bruner, Jerome. "The Role of Dialogue in Language Acquisition." *The Child's Conception of Language*. Ed. A. Sinclair. New York: Springer-Verlag, 1978.

Cintron, Ralph. "Reading and Writing Graffitti: A Reading." *The Quarterly Newsletter of the Laboratory of Comparative Human Cognition* 13 (1991): 21–24.

DiPardo, Anne. "Acquiring 'A Kind of Passport': The Teaching and Learning of Academic Discourse in Basic Writing Tutorials." Diss. UC Berkeley, 1991.

——. *'A Kind of Passport': A Basic Writing Adjunct Program and the Challenge of Student Diversity*. Urbana: NCTE, [1993.]

Dorris, Michael. *A Yellow Raft in Blue Water*. New York: Holt, 1987.

Dyson, Anne. "Weaving Possibilities: Rethinking Metaphors for Early Literacy Development." *The Reading Teacher* 44 (1990): 202–13.

Fischer, Michael. "Ethnicity and the Postmodern Arts of Memory." *Writing Culture: The Poetics and Politics of Ethnography*. Ed. J. Clifford and G.E. Marcus. Berkeley: U of California P, 1986.

Hawkins, Thom. "Intimacy and Audience: The Relationship Between Revision and the Social Dimension of Peer Tutoring." *College English* 42 (1980): 64–68.

Hull, Glynda, and Mike Rose. "Rethinking Remediation: Toward a Social-Cognitive Understanding of Problematic Reading and Writing." *Written Communication* 6 (1989): 139–54.

——. "This Wooden Shack: The Logic of an Unconventional Reading." *College Composition and Communication* 41 (1990): 287–98.

John, Vera P. "Styles of Learning—Styles of Teaching: Reflections on the Education of Navajo Children." *Functions of Language in the Classroom*. Ed. Courtney B. Cazden and Vera P. John. 1972. Prospect Heights: Waveland, 1985.

Locust, Carol. "Wounding the Spirit: Discrimination and Traditional American Indian Belief Systems." *Harvard Educational Review* 58 (1988): 315–30.

Philips, Susan U. "Participant Structures and Communicative Competence: Warm Springs Children in Community and Classroom." *Functions of Language in the Classroom*. Ed. Courtney B. Cazden and Vera P. John. 1972. Prospect Heights: Waveland, 1985.

Reichard, Gladys. *Social Life of the Navajo Indians*. 1928. New York: AMS P, 1969.

Shaughnessy, Mina. "Diving In: An Introduction to Basic Writing." *College Composition and Communication* 27 (1976): 234–39.

Terrell, John Upton. *The Navajo: The Past and Present of a Great People*. 1970. New York: Perennial, 1972.

Valdés, Guadalupe. *Identifying Priorities in the Study of the Writing of Hispanic Background Students*. Grant. No. OERI-G-008690004. Washington, DC: Office of Educational Research and Improvement, 1989.

——. *Language Issues in Writing: The Problem of Compartmentalization of Interest Areas Within CCCC*. Paper presented at the Conference on College Composition and Communication. 21–23 March, 1991.

Vygotsky, Lev. *Mind in Society*. Cambridge: Harvard UP, 1978.

RESPONDING TO TEXTS

Provocative Revision

Toby Fulwiler
UNIVERSITY OF VERMONT

Each tutor develops a philosophy of what tutoring should achieve. For Toby Fulwiler, "teaching writing is teaching re-writing," which involves teaching students how to revise their writing through the techniques of limiting, adding, switching, and transforming. "Early drafts by inexperienced writers try to cover too much territory," and tutors can be effective in helping students keep a topic to a manageable size and depth. In the process, tutors can "make the case that re-seeing writing in a different form is . . . generative, liberating, and fun." Fulwiler's essay, which originally appeared in The Writing Center Journal *in 1992, provides insights into revision as a major aspect of the composing process and offers support for the view that modeling the revision process for students can be constructive.*

I HAVE BEEN TEACHING WRITING FOR TWENTY-FOUR YEARS, first at the University of Wisconsin, later at Michigan Technological University, now at [the] University of Vermont. During the past fifteen years, I have also worked closely with writing centers, watching them evolve from places which emphasize skills and drills to places which provide sophisticated and supportive counseling about the range of writing processes. While my education is far from complete, I have learned what you too must know: that teaching writing is teaching re-writing.

During that same time, however, I have also learned that for novice writers, learning to re-write is an alien activity that doesn't come easily. In fact, many college students, first year and graduate alike, assume that writing is essentially copying down what they've already been thinking—well, maybe with a little spell checking, editing a few awkward sentences, adding a transition or two, and throwing in (get it, throwing in) a few supportive examples.

In contrast, I am convinced that revision is the primary way that both thinking and writing evolve, mature, and improve. So now, when I teach writing, I no longer leave revision to chance, happenstance, or writer whimsy. I not only encourage it, I provoke it, emphasizing where, when, and how to do it. At the same time, I go to great lengths to make sure the writing remains each student's own.

The rest of this paper is concerned with the *where, when,* and *how* of revision. I know how I, a classroom teacher who makes multiple-draft assignments, teach revision. What I am proposing to you who teach by tutoring is a set of provocative suggestions that will help your students learn to take revision seriously. These provocations are four: (1) limiting, (2) adding, (3) switching, and (4) transforming.

1. Limiting

Generalization is death to good writing. Limiting is the cure for generality. The problem with generalities is that most people already know the same ones you do. They get bored hearing them repeated again and again. Most people (a generality I make with some trepidation) who read newspapers and weekly news magazines or listen to TV or radio news know general things about famous people and current issues: that the President plays golf, that the crisis in the Middle East won't go away, that communism is on the run in Eastern Europe, as is the natural environment in the United States. What most people do not know about are the close-in details of these same specific issues—the telling details that make subjects come to life. One of the key qualities of writing that we might call "interesting" is that it teaches us something we did not already know—something beyond repetitious small-talk generality. Once a subject—be it a person, place, or problem—is explored through careful research and exposed through thoughtful writing, people are drawn in because they find themselves learning something new.

It's the details that teach. People are fascinated with the details of other people's lives and so biographies and autobiographies frequent the best-seller lists—stories about the details of Presidents and rock stars as well as the assassins who shoot them. In like manner, people are fascinated with details of problems: classic examples include Rachel Carson's detailed exposé of environment-destroying pesticides in *Silent Spring*; Ralph Nader's in-depth investigation of Chevrolet's Corvair in *Unsafe at Any Speed*; and Bob Woodward and Carl Bernstein's minute revelations about the Watergate scandal in *All the President's Men*. Likewise it's the details in the research essays published in current periodicals, from *Rolling Stone* to *The New Yorker*, that make those magazines fascinating to read.

But writers have only so much time to write and space to work with, and so to spend more time and space including details means not including something else—which is where the concept of *limiting* helps out. Here are some specific

suggestions for applying the principle of limiting to both narrative and research writing.

Limiting Time, Place, and Action   In narrative and personal experience papers, a writer's first instinct is to try to tell or summarize the whole story. Such
a generalized approach often gives the writer his or her first sense of what the
story is about. As a teacher of first-year and advanced writing classes, I have
come to expect—and accept as natural and useful—such overview writing on
first drafts. Here, for example, are recent samples of fairly typical openings in
first-draft narrative papers:

> This is probably the most heroic event of my childhood. Everyone has their mo-
> ments, but I believe that this episode is indeed commendable. . . .

> Life, it definitely has its ups and downs. Every so often I realize just what stupid,
> mindless things I've caught myself doing to fill time. . . .

> Last summer my mother and I flew to Ireland. . . . This action packed vacation
> turned out to be more than I could handle. From recalling old memories to falling
> in love, I helped discover a new side of myself. . . .

> In everyday life there are so many things that frustrate us or make us upset that
> when we find something that makes us truly happy, we should take advantage of
> it at every opportunity. . . .

> This is an experience I hope never to experience again in my lifetime. A friend
> of my parents committed suicide by shooting himself in the head. This hurt
> me a great deal because I was close to his children and I felt the pain they were
> feeling. . . .

These opening lines provide several clues to the problems typical of first-draft
narrative writing: first, these writers generalize rather than particularize their
experience, putting it into pre-packaged story categories (heroism, action-
adventure). Second, they evaluate their experience too early, prejudging it, and
telling readers in advance to react to it as stupid, frustrating, heroic, etc. Third,
though you cannot see this from one paragraph fragment, many writers don't
know in a first draft what their final-draft story will be. Consider, for example,
this passage from a first-draft essay by Amanda, a first-year student from Scot-
land, writing a paper entitled "Waitressing":

> For most of this summer I again worked on the farm, where I removed rotten,
> diseased potato shaws from a field all day. But I was in the sun all the time with a
> good bunch of people so it was quite good fun. But again it was hard work. (As are
> most jobs!) My waitressing job was nothing to get excited about either. I signed up
> with an employment agency and got a waitressing job in Aberdeen, a city thirty
> miles north of our farm. It was only for one week, but I didn't mind—it was the
> first job that I had got myself and I felt totally independent.

Were Amanda to focus close, this single paragraph could divide into two entirely
different directions, one focusing on her title topic, "Waitressing," and a second
on "Farming"—in particular, working the potato fields. In fact, this passage reveals

all three features typical of first-draft writing: over-generalizations, prejudgment, and directional uncertainty. The problem with such writing is not that it is wrong or incorrect, but that it seldom makes good reading. The solution is usually in the writer's returning to the piece, re-seeing it, looking more closely, and finding through continued exploration, the story that wants or needs to come out.

Although such revision sometimes happens by itself, especially for writers who are engaged in their task, it does not happen for writers who are not engaged, who are going through the motions of completing somebody else's task—a common predicament in school writing. But there are some ways to begin to create engagement, even in assignments the writer does not yet own. For example, with Amanda's class, I asked all the students to write two new pages about an idea covered in one first-draft paragraph. I was asking them, in other words, to radically and forcibly narrow their focus. Here is a brief portion of Amanda's next draft:

> [Harvesting potatoes] was always in October, so the weather was never very good. It either rained or was windy, often both. Some days it would be so cold that we would lie in between the drills of undug potatoes to protect ourselves from the wind.

In this draft, Amanda's details are helping her tell the story: notice especially the detail about lying "in between the drills of undug potatoes" to keep out of the wind. That's a *telling detail*, the detail that only a writer who has actually dug potatoes on a cold October day is likely to know—the detail that begins to tell the real story for her and to which she ought to listen very closely. Amanda has a lot to say about digging potatoes.

After witnessing the life and energy in the potato field draft, I suggested that Amanda revise again, not about what *usually* occurred in October, but about what *particularly* occurred one day in October. (Aristotle gave this same advice three thousand years ago in his *Poetics* and Robert Pirsig two decades ago in *Zen and the Art of Motorcycle Maintenance*.) I suggested, in other words, that Amanda start her next draft by limiting the *time, place,* and *action* of her potato field story; her next draft begins this way:

> Potatoes, mud, potatoes, mud, potatoes, that was all I saw in front of me. They moved from my right side to my left, at hip level. A conveyor belt never stopping. On and on and on.
>
> I bounced and stumbled around as the potato harvester moved over the rough earth, digging the newly grown potatoes out of the ground, transporting them up a conveyor belt and pushing them out in front of me and three other ladies, two on either side of the belt.
>
> The potatoes passed fast, a constant stream. My hands worked deftly, pulling out clods of dirt, rotten potatoes, old shaws, and anything else I found that wasn't a potato. They were sore, rubbed raw with the constant pressure of holding dirt. They were numb, partly from the work and partly from the cold. It was October, the ground was nearly frozen, the mud was hard and solid. Cold. Dirt had gotten into my yellow and yet brown rubber gloves, had wedged under my nails increasing my discomfort.
>
> On and on the tractor pulled the harvester I was standing in, looming high above the dark rich earth, high above the potatoes. . . .

In this, her third draft, Amanda found her story and, in finding it, she found the telling particulars that put us beside her in the potato harvester. The specific suggestion to limit the time frame of her story made all the difference and good writer though Amanda turned out to be, had the revision not been provoked, it wouldn't have happened.

Limiting Scope and Focus   A similar limiting principle also holds true for more analytical or objective writing. *All* first drafts are first explorations and, as such, are likely to be overly generalized, obviously editorialized, and directionally incomplete. As in narrative, so in exposition, argument, and research, early drafts by inexperienced writers try to cover too much territory. It's understandable and predictable. When writers do not yet know a lot about a subject, they see it as if from a distance—and from a distance, even cities and mountains look small and manageable. Writers of such drafts then have the choice of staying far away, letting the generalities stand, and moving on to new subjects (and usually to mediocre papers) or moving in close, narrowing and sharpening the focus, and doing real writer's work—which means exploring the geography up close.

When I assign research projects to my students, I suggest—nay, require— that, in addition to library research, they find some local dimension of their topic, issue, or problem worth investigating. If, for example, they plan to research the abortion question, can they visit the local Planned Parenthood or a pregnancy clinic? If they plan to research something related to the environment, can they visit the local lake, landfill, or development to see the problem first hand?

I need to explain here that when I assign research projects in first-year writing classes, I require that the collecting of information be collaborative, and I strongly recommend the writing be collaborative as well. I do this for several reasons: first, to reduce the harassment of local institutions and people; second, to make the information-collecting process more rapid and efficient; and third, to model collaborative writing so often required of writers in the world outside of college. Though writing center tutors seldom determine whether research writing should be individual or collaborative, be assured that the revision techniques described here work in either situation.

In one first-year writing class, a group of five students researched the rise of *Ben and Jerry's Ice Cream Company*—a local business developed by former University of Vermont students—and, in the following paragraph, described their visit to the original downtown store:

> To the left of the stairs is a long, brown wooden bench with black metal legs that looks like it came straight from Central Park. Above it, on the wall, is a blown-up article from the *Rutland Herald*. To the right of the bench is a white, metal wastebasket, three feet high and two feet wide. On top of the wastebasket is a blue bucket that says "We are now recycling spoons." On every table in the room are napkin dispensers saying, "Save a tree, please take only one napkin."

On the one hand, this is a simple example of on-site descriptive writing meant to give readers the feel of the ice cream store. On the other hand, the recycling signs provide readers with their first clue that "environmental awareness" will be a major theme in the *Ben and Jerry's* research report. Further in the report the authors include library-based research information:

> *Ben and Jerry's* is now looking for an alternative for their pint containers because they are made with a plastic coating for moisture resistance. This combination of materials makes the container non-biodegradable and difficult to recycle. According to their Annual Report, "As a result of this and other recycling efforts, we have reduced our solid waste volume by about 30% this year" (6).

The *Ben and Jerry's* paper concludes by arguing that profit making and environmental protection are not mutually exclusive—a thesis that emerged only gradually as the writers conducted their investigation and experimented with different drafts.

2. Adding

Perhaps the most obvious way to revise a paper is to add new information and more explanation. Most professional writers see adding and revising as synonymous. (They feel the same about subtracting and revising, but that's seldom the novice writer's problem.) However, few of the student writers who visit writing centers are likely to understand what addition could mean, unless an assignment has been made in multiple-draft stages, where proposals, outline, first and second drafts are required over a several week period. In any case, most students can profit by learning about addition, if they seek help early enough so there is time to do it. I want to illustrate this principle by continuing to emphasize local knowledge, this time recommending the addition of "dialogue"—people talking—to both personal experience and research writing.

Adding Dialogue   Having people talk in a paper adds interest by limiting the focus to one or two people or a particular scene. In narrative or personal-experience writing, adding dialogue complements Aristotle's suggestion to limit time, place, and action, by putting actors on the sets. Adding talk allows readers to see and hear a story in a dramatic rather than narrative way, increasing reader involvement and interest.

To add talk to narrative writing requires remembering what was said sometime in the past or, more likely, re-creating what was probably or approximately said. Fiction is not allowed, but approximate re-creation is fair game for all experiential or autobiographical writing.

For example, in response to an assignment to draft a personal-experience paper, Karen described her whole basketball season in three pages, concluding with the team playing in the Massachusetts semi-final game in the Boston Garden:

> We lost badly to Walpole in what turned out to be our final game. I sat on the bench most of the time. The coach did not even put me in until the fourth quarter when there were five minutes left and we were already twenty points behind.

For their second drafts, I asked these first-year writers to work dialogue into their narratives. Karen's second draft includes this scene:

"Girls, you have got to keep your heads in the game. Don't let them get you down. You've worked so hard all season. You are just as good as them, just look at our record, 18-2-0.

"Coach, they're killing us. They're making us look like fools, running right by us. We're down by twenty with eight minutes to go. It's hopeless."

"I don't want to hear anyone talk like that. You girls have worked too hard to get to this point and give up. You can't quit now."

Yeah, think of every sweat-dripping, physically-gruelling, suicide-sprinting, drill-conditioning Saturday morning practice this year. ("OK girls, for every missed foul shot it's one full suicide!") Oh, yes, I remember those practice sessions just fine.

"Tweet!"

Oh well, I missed another time out. It really doesn't matter, because he won't play me anyway.

Karen has added not only dialogue, but interior monologue as well, turning her paper from a summative to a dramatic telling. In this later version, we learn that Karen's dream changes from hoping her team will win the championship to sinking for herself a three-pointer in the Boston Garden—if only she can get into the game. Karen's second draft has expanded to six pages, but focuses only on the last eight minutes of the basketball game.

Adding Interviews Adding other voices also improves research writing—only now the adding requires actual on-site interviews in place of remembered or recreated dialogue. As a teacher of research, I've long been influenced by Ken Macrorie's notion of *I-Search Papers*, Eliot Wiginton's Foxfire stories—now up to twelve volumes—as well as the practices of investigative reporters who go places, ask questions, and record the results. Adding on-site information from experts increases a paper's credibility and readability at the same time.

One group of four first-year writing students investigated the role of the Ronald McDonald House in providing housing for out-of-town parents while their children stayed in hospitals. In Burlington, a Ronald McDonald House is located between downtown and the University of Vermont Medical Center, within walking distance of the UVM campus. A *Free Press* story turned up through library research reported the following information:

The McDonald's corporation actually provides about 5% of the total cost of getting the house started. The other 95% of the money comes from local businesses and special interest groups.

For their second draft, however, the group visited the house and interviewed parents, volunteer workers, and the director. In the following passage, Rosemary, the House director, explains the sources of funding:

"Our biggest problem is that people think we're supported by the McDonald's corporation. We have to get people to understand that anything we get from *McDonald's* is just from that particular franchise's generosity—and may be no more than is donated by other local merchants. *Martin's, Hood,* and *Ben and Jerry's* provide much of the food. *McDonald's* is not obligated to give us anything. The only reason we use their name is because of its child appeal."

Which information, that found in the library or that revealed through live interview, is the most useful for research writers? Which is more interesting or memorable for readers? No need to choose, for in their final draft, the writers included both pieces of information, the one written with statistical authority, the other spoken with personal authority. Adding the voices of real live local experts also holds true for other kinds of objective writing as well: when writers let other voices help them argue, report, and evaluate, their arguments, reports, etc., are both more persuasive and exciting.

3. Switching

Switching involves telling the same story or reporting the same events as the previous draft, but doing so from a different perspective. For example, if a writer has been narrating in past tense, she switches to present. If a writer has been reporting research results in third person, he switches to first person for all or part of a draft. Switching a basic element, such as tense or point-of-view, mechanically provokes writers into re-seeing the content and often into reconceptualizing how to present it with maximum effect.

Switching Point of View   In narrative and personal experience writing, the most common first-draft perspective is first person: "Once upon a time I was playing basketball" or something like this. It's only natural that writers tell stories as they experienced them, through their own eyes, perspectives, voices. However, it sometimes helps writers to move deliberately outside of themselves and see themselves as someone else might. This can be done simply by switching pronouns or, in a more complex way, by role-playing a third person. In the following example, Karen continues to tell her story of playing in the Massachusetts basketball semi-finals, but for this draft she adopts the perspective and voice of the play-by-play announcer:

> Well folks, it looks as if Belmont has given up. Coach Gleason is preparing to send in his subs. It has been a rough game for Belmont. They stayed in it during the first quarter, but Walpole has run away with it since then. Down by twenty with only six minutes left, Belmont's first sub is now approaching the bench.
>
> Megan Sullivan goes coast to coast and lays it in for two. She has sparked Walpole from the start.
>
> The fans have livened up a bit, but oddly they aren't Walpole's fans, they're Belmont's. Cheers for someone named Karen are coming from the balcony. . . . Number eleven, Karen Kelly replaces Michelle Hayes.

By becoming the announcer, Karen adopts the cadences and spirit of an announcer in the broadcast booth, seeing and reporting the game as she imagines he actually did. Whether the announcer would have paid even this much attention to a substitute player entering in the last few minutes of the game is questionable—but that's not the point. By adding this voice, Karen added more details and a different perspective to her own story. In this draft, she realizes for the first time that her basketball enemies were actually three: the opposing team, the coach who refused to play her, and also her teammates who refused to give her the ball.

Switching Voice   Another switch that provides new perspective on exposition or argument is changing the voice that's doing the explaining or arguing. For example, changing the voice that delivers the information from objective third person to subjective first changes the nature of the information as well as the way it is received. Furthermore, if we use as examples the research essays commonly published in leading non-fiction journals, we notice that writers such as Joan Didion, John McPhee, and Jonathan Kozol commonly write in more than one voice—or in one voice, but varying tones, pitches, and registers. Why can't student research writing gain life by using similar techniques?

Here, for example, in the final draft of a thirty-page research report written by a group of first-year writers about pollution in Lake Champlain are four different voices:

> [The Introduction is narrated by an out-of-town male student, who opens the report by meeting an in-town female student.]

> Page 1: We both started to cycle and I followed her down a path near the lake: "I'm just amazed by the beauty of the water. It is great to see the islands out there in front of us. This is paradise," I said.
> "Well, there are some problems with the lake. The sewage treatment plant," she paused and continued, "it's taken a lot of the beauty away."
> "What do you mean?" I asked, and she proceeded to tell me the story. . . .

> Page 3: How do you close down a public beach? You can't barricade the water, can you? *The Burlington Free Press* always used the word "Fecal Coliform," which basically means "shit." But the technological meaning is "a bacteria that indicates human waste." That almost sounds worse than shit!

> Page 7: The sewage treatment plant of Burlington consists of a series of wells, pumps, and tanks. It is built to receive forty million gallons of waste water from the street drainage sewers of private and public bathrooms. During large rain-storms, the amount of water causes difficulties in the plant's ability to treat all the water which enters it.

> Page 18: Some helpful hints for conserving water:

> 1. Take short showers. Get wet first, then turn the shower off, lather up, then turn the shower on and rinse off.

> 2. Don't keep the water running while you're brushing your teeth.

> 3. Keep a jug of drinking water cool in the refrigerator instead of running the tap water to get it cold.

In these selected passages, the writers keep reader interest by sometimes switching to unexpected voices. At the same time, the report delivers the goods, describing and explaining the problem of lake pollution from personal and technological perspectives, and offering a range of solutions that include both technological fixes and changing personal behavior.

4. Transforming

My final revision strategy is transforming, where a writer re-casts his or her piece into a form altogether different from what it has been. For example, if the piece has been drafted as something called a personal-experience paper, could it be recast as an exchange of letters or a diary? If a piece has been initially drafted as a formal research paper, could it be recast as a speculative or familiar essay? While these moves may seem, at best, superficial or, at worst, inappropriately playful for college-level work, I'd like to make the case that re-seeing writing in a different form is, at the same time, generative, liberating, and fun. Any time writers change around the way they present their ideas and information, they open up new conceptual possibilities in terms of both audience and purpose. In so doing, the staleness that sometimes accompanies routine acts of revision is relieved, and an excitement borne of experimentation takes over. Let me give you some final examples.

Transforming Research Reports Research papers are all too often the reports that students hate to write and faculty hate to read. Do they need to be that way—problems for both student writers and faculty readers—with tutors caught in the middle? Some of the students whose work I've already examined have found interesting solutions to this problem.

Remember the Ronald McDonald House? In their final draft, these four writers collaborated to write a script for *60 Minutes*. The form is, of course, fiction, but the content is the hard information uncovered through extensive local research. Here are some of the parts of the script:

[The opening paragraph of the "Editor's Note" which served as a preface to the script.]

In this documentary we had a few problems with getting certain interviews and information. As the house is a refuge for parents in distress, our questions were often limited. We didn't want to pry.

[The opening paragraph of the script.]

Smith: Hello, this is John Smith reporting for *60 Minutes*. Our topic for this week is the Ronald McDonald House. Here I am in front of the House in Burlington, Vermont, but before I go inside, let me fill you in on the history of this and many other houses like it. . . .

[Within the script are scenes called a "Camera Eye," set in boldface type, portraying the house from the objective view of the TV camera.]

Toward the back of the house, three cars and one camper are parked in an oval-shaped, gravel driveway. Up three steps onto a small porch are four black plastic chairs and a small coffee table. On top of a table is a black ashtray filled with crumpled cigarette butts.

[Smith learns about the house by going on a walking tour with a volunteer hostess named Robin; most of the information about the Ronald McDonald House comes from Robin's answers to Smith's questions.]

Smith: Do you always cook dinner for the families?
Robin: Oh no. Most of the time they cook their own meals. However, if we have free time, we might make something for them. It's really nice for them to come home to food on the stove.

In other words, rather than writing a report with no audience in mind, in the generic form of a term paper—which exists nowhere in the world outside of school—these writers posed the hypothetical problems faced by prime-time TV writers and imagined how they would solve them. Their simple idea of an "Editor's Note" is itself an interesting move: whereas in typical college research papers authors try to pretend they know everything, in this format the student writers felt they could be more candid about real problems they encountered and how it limited their resulting script.

Remember the group researching pollution in Lake Champlain? Their factual report is framed by a narrative story told by a fictional student; the report itself includes a tour of the waste treatment plant, interviews with merchants and shoppers to find out the level of public awareness of the problem, and statistical results from a self-designed survey given to Burlington residents about the pollution problem. The *Ben and Jerry's* report resulted in a feature article aimed for publication in *The Burlington Free Press*, complete with illustrations. And another group in the same class reported on the plight of the homeless in downtown Burlington and wrote their final paper as a short (twenty-page) book with five chapters, one by each writer, the last one collaborative.

Tutors need to be especially careful here in what you advise. Many professors who assign research projects will have a specific idea of what such reports should look like, and tutors need to be careful to counsel the student in those directions. However, if a student's professor is open to innovative approaches to the assignment, tutors might suggest that re-forming the final draft into something other than a term paper will be more creative, and fun to do, and interesting to read.

Reforming Narrative Remember Amanda and the story of the potato field? It turns out that the "mud, potatoes, mud, potatoes" draft we looked at earlier described her most recent work on her father's farm, after he had replaced manual labor with a mechanical harvester. In a subsequent draft, she wrote about the old days when up to sixty neighborhood people—men, women, children—had harvested the potatoes by hand:

> 1983. . . . I bent down to help Louise finish her stretch of newly uncovered potatoes. It was piece time. We had an hour to devour lunch before the next shift of potato picking began. . . . Martin, who worked alongside me and Louise, had uncovered a nest of field mice, so we saved them from being chopped up by the digger. They were so cute—I hope we got them all. . . .

In her final portfolio draft, Amanda's paper most resembles a drama in two acts, with one act set in 1983 when field hands dug the potatoes, and including large portions of dialogue. The second act, separated by extra white space, is set in 1988 when she worked inside the potato-harvesting machine, and takes place largely as an internal monologue ("Potatoes, mud, potatoes, mud. . ."). However, at the very end she also included a new piece of writing, a coda, set off by extra white space, which explained her final understanding of the story she once thought was about waitressing:

> 1989. This year the potato harvester is still working, the same women on board, with the same bored expressions on their faces. Soon this job will probably not need anyone to work or help the machinery. Labour is an expense farmers cannot afford. There are no tattie holidays anymore, no extra pocket money for the children of the district. Change, technology, development is what they say it is. I say it is a loss of valuable experience in hard work and a loss of good times.

In her final draft, Karen our basketball player, provides three scenes, two occurring simultaneously and one sequentially: first, the play-by-play from the announcer's point of view; second, her time on the bench and in the game; third, outside the locker room where she finds her father and they have a tearful celebratory conversation. Like Amanda, the third scene was generated only at the time of the final draft, adding a kind of closure to an eight-page story. (And, yes, Karen does make a three-point basket in the Boston Garden.)

It is interesting that Karen made extra copies of her basketball paper at Kinko's to give as Christmas presents to her family. But Amanda, who was equally proud of her potato story, did not send a copy home, so critical had she become of her father's decision to mechanize the harvesting of potatoes on the farm.

In the same class, John, who had been trying to write an essay covering his eleven months in Ecuador, re-formed his essay into a series of cuts from a diary spaced throughout the year—a form that allowed him to show intermittent slices of his growth, but skip long deadly summaries. In like manner, Avy, trying to describe a long distance friendship over a four-year period, recreated periodic telephone conversations to show the passing of time.

Prior to attending college, many of these writers had been trained to write five-paragraph themes in Advanced Placement English classes; what they discovered as they shaped and reshaped their stories was how much fun it was to write in forms they invented for themselves. Again, tutors need to be cautious in their counsel, but when they discover writers locked into one tedious way of telling their stories, tutors can find out if there is any room in the assignments—or time in their lives—for experimentation and play.

These are the techniques that provoke serious revision in novice writers, showing them specific moves while allowing them to retain ownership of their papers. With a little thoughtful and cautious modification, they may also work for tutors.

Minimalist Tutoring:
Making the Student Do All the Work

Jeff Brooks _____

SEATTLE PACIFIC UNIVERSITY

In presenting the philosophy of minimalist tutoring, Jeff Brooks argues that "the goal of each tutoring session is learning, not a perfect paper." In contrast to those who view the tutor as a proofreader and editor, Brooks sees the tutor as a commentator and guide and contends that "fixing flawed papers is easy; showing the students how to fix their papers is complex and difficult." Like Stephen North, he believes that the tutor's job is to improve the writer, not the writer's text; "our primary object in the writing center session is not the paper, but the student," he says. For tutors to achieve the goals of minimalist tutoring, Brooks advocates a hands-off approach to students' papers—one that avoids editing the papers for errors in favor of emphasizing structure, organization, logical reasoning, and stylistic control. He explains the assumptions that guide this model and describes the techniques and strategies of forms of minimalist tutoring that he terms "basic," "advanced," and "defensive." This essay first appeared in 1991 in Writing Lab Newsletter.

A WRITING CENTER WORST CASE SCENARIO: A student comes in with a draft of a paper. It is reasonably well-written and is on a subject in which you have both expertise and interest. You point out the mechanical errors and suggest a number of improvements that could be made in the paper's organization; the student agrees and makes the changes. You supply some factual information that will strengthen the paper; the student incorporates it. You work hard, enjoy yourself, and when the student leaves, the paper is much improved. A week later, the student returns to the writing center to see you: "I got an A! Thanks for all your help!"

This scenario is hard to avoid, because it makes everyone involved feel good: the student goes away happy with a good grade, admiring you; you feel intelligent, useful, helpful—everything a good teacher ought to be. Everything about it seems right. That this is bad points out the central difficulty we confront as tutors: we sit down with imperfect papers, but our job is to improve their writers.

When you "improve" a student's paper, you haven't been a tutor at all; you've been an editor. You may have been an exceedingly good editor, but you've been of little service to your student. I think most writing center tutors agree that we must not become editors for our students and that the goal of each tutoring session is learning, not a perfect paper. But faced with students who want us to "fix" their papers as well as our own desire to create "perfect" documents, we often find it easier and more satisfying to take charge, to muscle in on the student's paper, red pen in hand.

To avoid that trap, we need to make the student the primary agent in the writing center session. The student, not the tutor, should "own" the paper and take full responsibility for it. The tutor should take on a secondary role, serving mainly to keep the student focused on his own writing. A student who comes to the writing center and passively receives knowledge from a tutor will not be any closer to his own paper than he was when he walked in. He may leave with an improved paper, but he will not have learned much.

A writing teacher or tutor cannot and should not expect to make student papers "better"; that is neither our obligation, nor is it a realistic goal. The moment we consider it our duty to improve the paper, we automatically relegate ourselves to the role of editor.

If we can't fix papers, is there anything left for us to do? I would like to suggest that when we refuse to edit, we become more active than ever as educators. In the writing center, we have the luxury of time that the classroom teacher does not have. We can spend that time talking and listening, always focusing on the paper at hand. The primary value of the writing center tutor to the student is as a living human body who is willing to sit patiently and help the student spend time with her paper. This alone is more than most teachers can do, and will likely do as much to improve the paper as a hurried proofreader can. Second, we can talk to the student as an individual about the one paper before us. We can discuss strategies for effective writing and principles of structure, we can draw students' attention to features in their writing, and we can give them support and encouragement (writing papers, we shouldn't forget, is a daunting activity).

Assumptions

All of this can be painfully difficult to do. Every instinct we have tells us that we must work for perfection; likewise, students pressure us in the same direction. I have found two assumptions useful in keeping myself from editing student papers:

1. The most common difficulty for student writers is paying attention to their writing. Because of this, student papers seldom reflect their writers' full capabilities. Writing papers is a dull and unrewarding activity for most students, so they do it in noisy surroundings, at the last minute, their minds turning constantly to more pressing concerns. It is little wonder that so much student writing seems haphazard, unfocused, and disorganized. A good many errors are made that the student could easily have avoided. If we can get students to reread a paper even once before handing it in, in most cases we have rendered an improvement. We ought to encourage students to treat their own writings as texts that deserve the same kind of close attention we usually reserve for literary texts.

Our message to students should be: "Your paper has value as a piece of writing. It is worth reading and thinking about like any other piece of writing."

2. While student writings are texts, they are unlike other texts in one important way: the process is far more important than the product. Most "real-world" writing has a goal beyond the page; anything that can be done to that writing to make it more effective ought to be done. Student writing, on the other hand, has no real goal beyond getting it on the page. In the real world when you need to have something important written "perfectly," you hire a professional writer; when a student hires a professional writer, it is a high crime called plagiarism.

This fairly obvious difference is something we often forget. We are so used to real-world writing, where perfection is paramount, that we forget that students write to learn, not to make perfect papers. Most writing teachers probably have a vision of a "perfect" freshman paper (it probably looks exactly like the pieces in the readers and wins a Bedford prize); we should probably resign ourselves to the fact that we will seldom see such a creature. Most students simply do not have the skill, experience, or talent to write the perfect paper.

Basic Minimalist Tutoring

Given these assumptions, there are a number of concrete ways we can put theory into practice. Our body language will do more to signal our intentions (both to our students and to ourselves) than anything we say. These four steps should establish a tone that unmistakably shows that the paper belongs to the student and that the tutor is not an editor.

1. Sit beside the student, not across a desk—that is where job interviewers and other authorities sit. This first signal is important for showing the student that you are *not* the person "in charge" of the paper.
2. Try to get the student to be physically closer to her paper than you are. You should be, in a sense, an outsider, looking over her shoulder while she works on her paper.
3. If you are right-handed, sit on the student's right; this will make it more difficult for you to write on the paper. Better yet, don't let yourself have a pencil in your hand. By all means, if you must hold something, don't make it a red pen!
4. Have the student read the paper aloud to you, and suggest that he hold a pencil while doing so. Aside from saving your eyes in the case of bad handwriting, this will accomplish three things. First, it will bypass that awkward first few moments of the session when you are in complete control of the paper and the student is left out of the action while you read his paper. Second, this will actively involve the student in the paper, quite likely for the first time since he wrote it. I find that many students are able to find and correct usage errors, awkward wording, even

logic problems without any prompting from me. Third, this will help establish the sometimes slippery principle that good writing should sound good.

I am convinced that if you follow these four steps, even if you do nothing else, you will have served the student better than you would if you "edited" his paper.

Advanced Minimalist Tutoring

Of course, there is quite a bit more you can do for the student in the time you have. You can use your keen intelligence and fine critical sense to help the student without directing the paper. As always, the main goal is to keep the student active and involved in the paper. I have three suggestions:

1. Concentrate on success in the paper, not failure. Make it a practice to find something nice to say about every paper, no matter how hard you have to search. This isn't easy to do; errors are what we usually focus on. But by pointing out to a student when he is doing something right, you reinforce behavior that may have started as a felicitous accident. This also demonstrates to the student that the paper is a "text" to be analyzed, with strengths as well as weaknesses. This is where the tutor can radically depart from the role of editor.

2. Get the student to talk. It's her paper; she is the expert on it. Ask questions—perhaps "leading" questions—as often as possible. When there are sentence-level problems, make the student find and (if possible) correct them. When something is unclear, don't say, "This is unclear"; rather, say, "What do you mean by this?" Instead of saying, "You don't have a thesis," ask the student, "Can you show me your thesis?" "What's your reason for putting Q before N?" is more effective than "N should have come before Q." It is much easier to point out mistakes than it is to point the student toward finding them, but your questions will do much more to establish the student as sole owner of the paper and you as merely an interested outsider.

3. If you have time during your session, give the student a discrete writing task, then go away for a few minutes and let him do it. For instance, having established that the paper has no thesis, tell the student to write the thesis while you step outside for a few minutes. The fact that you will return and see what he has accomplished (or not accomplished) will force him to work on the task you have given him probably with more concentration than he usually gives his writing. For most students, the only deadline pressure for their paper is the teacher's final due date. Any experienced writer knows that a deadline is the ultimate energizer. Creating that energy for a small part of the paper is almost the best favor you can do for a student.

Defensive Minimalist Tutoring

So far, I have been assuming that the student is cooperative or at least open to whatever methods you might use. This, of course, is not a very realistic assumption. There are many students who fight a non-editing tutor all the way. They know you know how to fix their paper, and that is what they came to have done. Some find ingenious ways of forcing you into the role of editor: some withdraw from the paper, leaving it in front of you; some refuse to write anything down until you tell them word for word what to write; others will keep asking you questions ("What should I do here? Is this part okay?"). Don't underestimate the abilities of these students; they will fatigue you into submission if they can.

To fight back, I would suggest we learn some techniques from the experts: the uncooperative students themselves.

1. Borrow student body language. When a student doesn't want to be involved in his paper, he will slump back in his chair, getting as far away from it as possible. If you find a student pushing you too hard into editing his paper, physically move away from it—slump back into your chair or scoot away. If a student is making a productive session impossible with his demands, yawn, look at the clock, rearrange your things. This language will speak clearly to the student: "You cannot make me edit your paper."

2. Be completely honest with the student who is giving you a hard time. If she says, "What should I do here?" you can say in a friendly, non-threatening way, "I can't tell you that—it's your grade, not mine," or, "I don't know—it's *your* paper." I have found this approach doesn't upset students as it might seem it would; they know what they are doing, and when you show that you know too, they accept that.

All of the suggestions I have made should be just a beginning of the ideas we can use to improve our value to our students. I hope that they lead to other ideas and tutoring techniques.

The less we do *to* the paper, the better. Our primary object in the writing center session is not the paper, but the student. Fixing flawed papers is easy; showing the students how to fix their own papers is complex and difficult. Ideally, the student should be the only active agent in improving the paper. The tutor's activity should focus on the student. If, at the end of the session, a paper is improved, it should be because the student did all the work.

Collaboration and Ethics
in Writing Center Pedagogy

*Irene Lurkis Clark*_____
UNIVERSITY OF SOUTHERN CALIFORNIA

Serving as a counterpoint to Jeff Brooks's essay on minimalist tutoring, Irene Clark's essay, which originally appeared in The Writing Center Journal *in 1988, validates a tutor's active collaboration with a student—including proofreading and editing for errors when instructive. She calls on tutors to be flexible in deciding what they will or will not do for students and to avoid entrenched policies. Citing the benefits of modeling writing tasks for students and the role of imitation in learning, she questions the pedagogical soundness of forbidding tutors to correct errors or rephrase passages. Clark traces the reluctance of theorists to endorse such help to paranoia about plagiarism and misplaced concern about how other depart- ments perceive writing centers. In urging tutors to avoid setting rigid rules against editing papers, Clark points to a colleague whose "graceful coherent style" is the result of a tutor at a British university who "would cross out any awkward sentences he found and replace them with more felicitous wording." Acting essentially as an apprentice to the tutor, Clark's colleague incorporated the tutor's technique and diction to form a style of his own. Clark finds such collaboration not only ethical but practical. She advocates true, collegial collaboration, however, which means not letting tutors "do the preponderance of the student's work."*

THE TERM COLLABORATIVE LEARNING has become well known only over the last fifteen years, but collaboration among academic colleagues has long been a part of university life. In the process of writing this paper, for example, I sub- mitted an early draft to my colleague, Betty Bamberg, who recommended that I write a new introduction, suggested an important additional source, and even noted a few typos. I, myself, regularly review the early drafts of book chapters for another colleague, and, on a few occasions, I have even rewritten a few sentences for him. Friends of mine in the social sciences assist one another even more regularly, suggesting sources, trading drafts, rephrasing and deleting sentences, polishing style. When an article is published, the author may write a formal note acknowledging the assistance of a colleague. But few of us worry about the ethics of such assistance or about whether this type of collegial collaboration could be viewed as a form of plagiarism.

In writing labs and centers, though, the kind of assistance which occurs regu- larly among colleagues might raise questions, if not eyebrows, over issues of ethics. In the writing center, tutors are usually not encouraged to make stylistic revisions or write on a student paper; in fact, only a student is supposed to even hold the pen. Nor are tutors supposed to suggest specific additional sources for reference. "You might go to the library and find some additional sources," a tutor might venture. Or else, "Do you think this section might be expanded? In what way?" In the context of writing center pedagogy, a tutor would be cautioned against rephrasing a student's sentence, nor would a tutor be encouraged to pass along one of his own articles for a student to look at for additional ideas or sources. After all, to give a student something written by a tutor might encourage plagiarism, either deliberate or inadvertent; and, certainly, one of the prime concerns of writing centers is to avoid charges of plagiarism at all costs. Unfortunately, however, writing centers' concern with avoiding charges of plagiarism and with self-justification in general have generated policies, which, in some instances, may actually be counterproductive to student learning.

In this context, then, I would like to address the following questions:

> Why are writing centers so concerned with issues of plagiarism?
> How has concern with plagiarism influenced writing center pedagogy?
> To what extent has this concern with plagiarism been counterproductive to student learning?

I first became aware of how suspiciously writing centers could be viewed by other departments when I gave a presentation in New Zealand several years ago. The purpose of my presentation was to explain how writing labs and centers functioned in the United States, and I approached my topic with great confidence and enthusiasm. However, I was surprised and dismayed to discover that several members of the faculty I was addressing were less than excited with my approach, feeling that any assistance a student received from a writing center tutor constituted a blatant form of plagiarism. "The students must love your center," one professor observed drily. "You do all of their work for them."

Of course, one might dismiss such an attitude as a misconception of the unenlightened. However, even a casual glance at writing center publications suggests that avoiding charges of plagiarism and justifying writing center pedagogy constitute a prime concern for writing center directors, suggesting that such suspicions are more widespread than is generally recognized. Larry Rochelle's article, appearing in the September 1981 issue of the *Writing Lab Newsletter*, observes the following:

> We must keep in mind that some "enemies" of the Center are overwrought English professors, our own colleagues, who really do not like students or teaching, who are very demanding in their classrooms for all the wrong reasons, and who really think that Writing Centers are helping students too much. (7)

The use of the word *enemies* here suggests that writing centers must remain alert to an attack of some sort, a state of mind more suggestive of the military than the university. Another article by Patrick Sullivan, appearing in the May 1984 issue of the *Newsletter*, similarly observes that the close relationships which develop between tutors and students sometimes generate their own "special set of problems. The instructor may not be aware that a student has received help with a writing assignment. In this case, instructors may feel that matters related to the policy of plagiarism obtain" (2). In a later *Writing Lab*

Newsletter article (December 1985), Sullivan discusses the results of a survey of faculty reaction to their students' receiving assistance from a writing center. Although many were pleased, even enthusiastic, about this sort of assistance, a surprising number regarded it with great mistrust. "I don't approve of them editing final drafts," one respondent observed. Another indicated that he highly disapproved of writing center assistance, particularly "in cases where a student has serious grammatical and organizational problems. I would even prefer he or she not take a draft of the paper to the Center at all, but rather get help through the use of verb exercises" (6). Again, this statement may be dismissed as yet another aberrant opinion; nevertheless, such a position is more common than we would like to believe.

Why are writing center teachers and administrators so concerned with the issue of plagiarism, more concerned, I would venture to guess, than those who work in language or math labs? One possible explanation is that writing, as opposed to other disciplines, has always been viewed as a solitary rather than as a collaborative activity, and therefore collaboration in any form is regarded with mistrust. In a recent CCCC presentation concerned with ethics and the writing center, Karen Hodges discussed the wide diversity in attitude toward collaborative effort among various disciplines, concluding that English departments, unlike departments in the natural and social sciences, were most concerned about the shaping of the text and thus were least likely to favor collaboration between student and professor.

Hodges maintained that because English departments tended to view content and form as interrelated, they were more suspicious of writing center pedagogy than departments in the sciences or social sciences. Sharing this perspective, Trimbur points out that the cultural history of writing suggests that writing a paper, as opposed to studying for an exam, has always been done on an individual basis. Referring to his own participation in study groups as an undergraduate, Trimbur states, "If Western Civilization was seen as a collective problem permitting a collective response, writing was apparently an individual problem, private and displaced from the informal network of mutual aid" (2). Similarly, Bruffee points out that "collaboration and community activity is inappropriate and foreign to work in humanistic disciplines, such as English. Humanistic study, we have been led to believe, is a solitary act" (645).

The humanities tradition dictates, then, that form and style, not simply content, are the essence of a text, and thus that writers, and in particular student writers, ought to work alone. The literature tells us of lonely poets and fiction writers inspired by muses at midnight; no one ever hears of a muse inspiring groups of two or three. Thus, any form of collaborative writing is open to suspicion, and writing centers, relatively new facilities within the university, are particularly concerned with being above suspicion and establishing their worth in order to wrangle funds out of dubious administrators. Neulieb's article in the March 1980 issue of the *Writing Lab Newsletter* highlights this concern with self-justification: "Proving to the university in general, and to those with the pursestrings in particular, that a writing facility has been effective and useful

takes a plan of action that includes several different thrusts" (2). Neulieb
continues that what is needed above all are

> . . . good press and visibility. Writing Lab staff have to be willing to come when
> called. . . . If a dean calls with a question about what to do with a split infinitive,
> even if his problem is just a divided compound verb, the Center had better be
> able to answer the question. If an education teacher gives his students in pri-
> mary education a test on language arts and finds out that they all think that the
> eight parts of speech include predicates, the Center had better be able to help
> those potential teachers. . . . As the eighties begin and enrollments shrink, we will
> be called on more and more often to prove our worth. (2-3)

Once again, one has the sense of "enemies" all around, of a self-defensiveness
and insecurity more characteristic of an underling than of a professional. Somehow, it seems unlikely that professionals in other fields—doctors, lawyers, engineers, even English scholars—would feel as if they had "better" be willing to
come when called or be willing to be on call for a split infinitive. The feeling one
gets from this passage is that writing centers are perpetually on the line and
could be phased out of existence for even one mistake.

Paranoia of this sort, however one might understand and identify with it, has
pedagogical implications which can be less than advantageous for both tutors
and students. For tutors, such excessive concern with self-justification and issues of plagiarism has generated insecurity about what is actually meant by collaboration and about what sort of assistance they ought to provide. As Trimbur
points out, tutoring is "a balancing act that asks tutors to juggle roles, to shift
identity, to know when to act like an expert and when to act like a co-learner"
(25), and the proper balance can only occur when a true writing community is
created. As Bruffee says, peer tutoring means that tutors and students talk to
each other about writing and learn to write as those in the community of literate
people write. "They talk about the subject and about the assignment. They talk
through the writer's understanding of the subject" (645). However, overconcern
with issues of ethics often results in a withholding and a rigidity which inhibits
the creation of a writing community and is antithetical to the flexibility which
ought to characterize a collaborative environment.

Such rigidity is highlighted in a *Writing Lab Newsletter* article published in
June 1983 in which Suzanne Edwards discusses several precepts she adheres to
in training her tutoring staff, precepts which are actually admonitions. Edwards'
first injunction is not to "write any portion of the paper—not even one phrase."
Another is for tutors *never* to "edit the paper for mechanical errors. This includes finding or labeling the spelling, punctuation, or grammar mistakes in a
paper or dictating corrections" (8). Similarly, at a recent conference, I over-
heard a colleague assert that she trains her tutors *never* to hold the pen or
pencil. Another colleague agreed, saying that at her center tutors *never* proof-
read papers. Unfortunately, writing center policies seem to be characterized by
a large number of "nevers."

Tutors at my own center as well have their share of *nevers*. Just the other day, one of my tutors said proudly that she *never* corrects a student's spelling; rather, she points out where the spelling mistakes are and has the student look them up in the dictionary. Otherwise, she felt, students would be given an unfair advantage. After all, she asked disdainfully, "Why should I act as a human spell-checker?" Another tutor agreed emphatically, adding that he does the same for punctuation.

Of course, in most instances, the underlying aim of policies such as these is not simply to protect the writing center from charges of plagiarism, but rather to enable students to become independent writers and learners, capable of generating and evaluating text on their own. From what learning theorists say, students learn best when they discover methods and ideas for themselves, when they are active participants in the learning process, not passive recipients of information. According to Jerome Bruner, "to instruct someone in [a] discipline is not a matter of getting him to commit results to mind. Rather it is to teach him to participate in the process that makes possible the establishment of knowledge. . . . Knowledge is a process, not a product" (72). In his discussion of tutoring, Bruner further asserts that "the tutor must direct his instruction in a fashion that eventually makes it possible for the student to take over the corrective function himself. Otherwise, the result of instruction is to create a form of mastery that is contingent upon the perpetual presence of the tutor" (53).

What seems to be overlooked in Bruner's discussion, however, are the implications of the term *eventually*. There is no question that the goal of writing centers is to make students ultimately independent of the assistance of a tutor. But perhaps during the early phases of the learning process, it might be beneficial for the tutor to assume a more active role. According to Vygotsky in his work on the relationship between development and learning in children, the most important learning occurs when teachers work with students at the "zone of proximal development," which he defines as "the distance between the actual developmental level as determined by independent problem solving and the level of potential development as determined through problem solving under adult guidance or in collaboration with more capable peers" (86). Thus, in terms of writing center pedagogy, in order for tutors to help students improve as writers, they should work on "functions that have not yet matured, but are in the process of maturation, functions that will mature tomorrow, but are currently in an embryonic state" (86). Such functions might well require more assistance from a tutor during the initial phase, but such input does not necessarily mean that the student is not learning how to perform the task himself or would be incapable of performing a similar task at a later time. As Vygotsky asserts, "what children can do with the assistance of others might be in some sense even more indicative of their mental development than what they can do alone" (85). Unlike primates, human beings "can imitate a variety of actions that go well beyond the limits of their own capabilities" (88).

Vygotsky maintains that "a full understanding of the concept of the zone of proximal development must result in reevaluation of the role of imitation in learning" (87); however, as Anne Gere points out, our culture is characterized by a "predisposition against imitation," which manifests itself as a "continuing resistance to collaborative work among writers" (4). In the past, though, imitation was a respected teaching method—at certain times, the method of choice. Referring to the development of oratory, Gere cites Isocrates' idea that the teacher "must in himself set such an example that the students who are molded by him are able to imitate him will, from the outset, show in their speaking a degree of grace and charm greater than that of others" (Gere 8). Cicero takes this idea one step further, asserting that through imitation, true evolution in oratory style occurs, enabling it to improve. To make this argument, "Cicero insists upon the stylistic individuality of orators who, having selected appropriate models and concentrated on their best features, improve upon what they imitate" (Gere 8). Quintilian also recommends imitation as the most effective means of developing oratory, but departs from Cicero in his recommendation to "paraphrase because of its challenge to achieve expression independent of the original" (Gere 10). In this regard, imitation may be viewed as ultimately creative, enabling the imitator to expand previous, perhaps ineffective models into something more effective which ultimately becomes his or her own. In the writing center, though, the arena in which such imitative experimentation could take place, excessive concern with plagiarism and self-protection prohibits this kind of modeling from taking place.

If we in writing centers were not so paranoid about charges of plagiarism, we would be more likely to avail ourselves of the pedagogical advantages of imitation. Thinking in terms of the "zone of proximal development," tutors might find it useful to "show" a student how to develop examples, correct an awkward sentence, maybe rephrase something, even help a student with a few spelling corrections. No doubt we all want students to learn to check their own spelling errors, but I think that supplying a correct spelling on occasion is unlikely to inhibit this learning. In response to my own tutor who did not want to be "a human spell-checker," I cited the numbers of students who seem to benefit from spell-checkers on their computers and suggested that, for a student who has never learned how to go through a text checking for spelling errors, watching a tutor do it could be very helpful. Certainly, forbidding this sort of assistance and generally creating a set of "injunctions" or "prohibitions" as part of established writing center policy do not seem pedagogically sound. More importantly, policies of this sort should not be made without a great deal of reflection concerning their impact on student learning.

After all, where did we acquire our own style in the first place? Surely none of us are under the impression that we actually "own" a particular phrase in the sense that we were the ones who had originated it. Sometimes the suggestion of a phrase or two can be wonderfully instructive, particularly for a foreign student; often a timely suggestion of a phrase can result in the student's adoption of that phrase as his or her own. A respected, well-published professor I know claims that his graceful coherent style is due to his undergraduate tutor at a British university. Apparently, each time he submitted a paper, the tutor would cross out any awkward sentences he found and replace them with more felicitous wording. As a student, he would faithfully imitate the style and language of his tutor, and, eventually, the tutor's suggestions became part of his own style. Apparently, in this situation, the tutor regarded the student as a potential colleague and was not particularly worried about plagiarism.

In his essay, "Ethics of Peer Tutoring," Gary Lichtenstein raises questions concerning the value of "defensive assertions," which are often characteristic of writing center policies, emphasizing that ethics should be considered only "in terms of the responsibilities of the tutor to the student" (33). Conceivably, such responsibility might at times involve "showing" a student how to accomplish a particular task, engaging students in conversation so that through listening and modeling they can apprehend the language of the culture. Muriel Harris maintains that "the non-directive approach rests on the assumption that most people can help themselves if they are freed from emotional obstacles such as fear of criticism and fear of failure" (70), an idea which is valid a good part of the time. However, there are numerous occasions on which students will not be able to help themselves, despite freedom from emotional obstacles, simply because they are unfamiliar with a certain genre, register, or mode of development, and no amount of circumspect questioning is going to enable them to perform the task correctly.

Without excessive concern about plagiarism, writing center tutors would be able to experiment with imitation as a pedagogical method—showing students how to develop examples, write introductions, and vary sentence structure. Concerning the injunction against proofreading, I can see that at certain times it might be very helpful for a student, especially a foreign student, to observe how a tutor goes through a paper, noting and correcting errors, perhaps reading aloud to sense the melody of the prose or reading backwards to check for typos. Moreover, in this situation, it would not be unreasonable for the tutor to hold the pen and even to use it occasionally to write on a student paper. With the student in attendance, the tutor could illustrate how text can be manipulated and moved, on the computer or with scissors and tape. Combing a text for one more example in a literary analysis, finding a model of a movie review in a newspaper—numerous writing techniques we have developed for ourselves can be acquired by students through the use of imitation and modeling.

In a recent CCCC presentation, Barry Kroll raised some interesting questions about the traditional arguments against plagiarism, pointing out that the notion that plagiarism is counterproductive to learning is not always true. "What happens," Kroll asks,

> if one comes to suspect that plagiarism (particularly the familiar case of copying a paragraph or so from a source) does not inevitably damage learning—at least no more seriously than *quoting* the same passage would damage learning. In fact, from the view of consequences to oneself, there would seem to be no morally significant difference between quoting and copying without acknowledgement: neither is more or less likely to lead to creativity, to learning, or to independent

thought. And what if one could show that copying a passage from a source sometimes leads to learning or improved writing? (5)

Of course, neither Kroll nor I feel that blatant plagiarism in any form can be justified by its potential benefit for student learning, even if such benefit could be demonstrated. My concern at this time is that we in writing centers retain a critical perspective on what has become part of established writing center policy, so that excessive prohibitions against certain forms of assistance do not become rigidly enshrined, accepted without question.

Dutifully, we all wax poetic about the benefits of collaborative learning. Yet, to a certain extent, true collaboration can occur only when collaborators are members of the same community—departmental colleagues, for instance, such as Betty and myself. True collaborators respond to one another honestly and do not withhold information from one another about trivial aspects of a paper (spelling, typos, missing commas, for example) because they fear providing too much assistance. In fact, one might venture that the more information withheld from a student and the more a tutor refrains from presenting information he knows, the more he is acting like a traditional teacher and the less likely it is that true collaboration will occur. After all, only teachers, not colleagues, ask questions to which they already know the answers. A recent study by Sarah Freedman suggests that tutors tend to give more expository explanations to higher-achieving students, who seem to elicit them by their comments and questions. My feeling is that with such higher-achieving students, the tutor behaves more like a peer than when he deliberately withholds ideas and information, whatever his pedagogical rationale might be.

Nevertheless, a qualification that must also be kept in mind is that the term *collaboration* suggests the idea of a true partnership. Thus, I am certainly not advocating that the tutor do the preponderance of the student's work, although, as we all know, that is exactly what some students would have us do. Rather, my concern is to raise critical questions about what has become entrenched as writing center policy, questions which are similar to those raised by Lisa Ede in a recent CCCC presentation. "Why have we as a profession been so obsessed with the fear that our students might plagiarize?" Ede queries. "Why have we clung so fervently to the notion of authorship as inherently individual?" (9). It is time, I believe, that we in writing centers stop worrying so much about what other departments will say about our work and devote ourselves to far more noteworthy goals—to establishing a writing environment characterized by flexibility and inquiry so that true collaborative effort can flourish.

Works Cited

Bruffee, Kenneth. "Collaborative Learning and the Conversation of Mankind." *College English* 46 (1984): 635-52.

Bruner, Jerome. *Toward a Theory of Instruction.* Cambridge: Belknap of Harvard UP, 1966.

Ede, Lisa. "The Case for Collaboration." Paper given at the Conference on College Composition and Communication. Atlanta, March 1987.

Edwards, Suzanne. "Tutoring Your Tutors." *Writing Lab Newsletter* June 1983: 7-9.

Freedman, Sarah, and Melanie Sperling. "Written Language Acquisition: The Role of Response and the Writing Conference." *The Acquisition of Written Language: Response and Revision.* Ed. Sarah W. Freedman. Norwood, N.J.: Ablex, 1985.

Gere, Ann Ruggles. "On Imitation." Paper given at the Conference on College Composition and Communication. Atlanta, March 1987.

Harris, Muriel. *Teaching One-to-One: The Writing Conference.* Urbana: NCTE, 1986.

Hodges, Karen. "The Writing of Dissertations: Collaboration and Ethics." Paper given at the Conference on College Composition and Communication. Atlanta, March 1987.

Kroll, Barry. "Why is Plagiarism Wrong?" Paper given at the Conference on College Composition and Communication. Atlanta, March 1987.

Lichtenstein, Gary. "The Ethics of Peer Tutoring." *The Writing Center Journal* 4.1 (1983): 29–35.

Neulieb, Janice. "Proving We Did It." *Writing Lab Newsletter* March 1980: 2–4.

Rochelle, Larry. "The ABC's of Writing Centers." *Writing Lab Newsletter* Sept. 1981: 7–9.

Sullivan, Patrick. "The Politics of the Drop-In Writing Center." *Writing Lab Newsletter* May 1984: 1–2.

Trimbur, John. "Peer Tutoring: A Contradiction in Terms?" *The Writing Center Journal* 7.2 (1987): 21–28.

Vygotsky, L. S. *Mind in Society: The Development of Higher Psychological Processes.* Cambridge: Harvard UP, 1978.

AFFIRMING DIVERSITY

Rethinking Writing Center Conferencing Strategies for the ESL Writer

Judith K. Powers

UNIVERSITY OF WYOMING

Judith Powers states that collaborative approaches that tutors use to good effect with native writers often fail when applied to ESL writers, who bring to the writing center different cultural values, needs, rhetorical strategies, and attitudes toward the tutor-student relationship. For example, the minimalist technique of having students read their papers aloud so that they can "hear" when diction or organizational problems arise does not appear to work for ESL writers. As a consequence, tutors may have to intervene more directly in ESL writers' texts, acting less as collaborators than as "informants." Powers makes a strong case for what she calls the need for an "attitude adjustment" on the part of writing center tutors when it comes to assisting ESL writers; tutors will find her article, which first appeared in 1993 in The Writing Center Journal, *especially helpful in making such an adjustment.*

THE UNIVERSITY OF WYOMING WRITING CENTER has recently experienced a dramatic increase in ESL conferencing, brought about mainly by the establishment of a writing across the curriculum program on campus and by changes in the way we teach first-year composition courses for international students. In responding to the almost three-fold increase in numbers of ESL conferences over the past two years, our writing center faculty has begun to question whether traditional collaborative strategies are appropriate and effective for second-language writers.

Probably more than anything else, the past two years' influx of ESL writers has pointed up two significant—and interrelated—concerns to writing center faculty. The first is how firm our assumptions are about our job and the "right" way to accomplish it. The second is how little training we as a faculty have in the principles and techniques of effective ESL conferencing. On both counts, we probably do not differ greatly from writing center faculties across the country. This paper presents the problems we encountered in conferencing with ESL writers and discusses the processes that evolved as we sought solutions.[1]

Traditional Conferencing Strategies and the ESL Writer

Since our writing center faculty was largely untrained in teaching ESL writing and unaware of the many differences in acquiring first- and second-language writing skills, the increase in numbers of ESL conferences proved a mixed blessing. We were delighted, on the one hand, to be reaching a greater number of second-language writers on campus; on the other hand, we sometimes felt frustrated when these conferences did not work the way we expected. Unfortunately, many of the collaborative techniques that had been so successful with native-speaking writers appeared to fail (or work differently) when applied to ESL conferences.

When ESL writers came into the writing center, we tended to approach those conferences just as we would conferences with native-speaking writers, determining what assistance the writers needed through a series of questions about process and problems, purpose and audience. In both cases, our intention in adopting this strategy was to establish a Socratic rather than a didactic context, one which we hoped would allow us to lead writers to the solution of their own problems. Occasionally, conferences might involve the direct exchange of information (e.g., when numbers should be spelled out). More typically, though, we intended to lead writers to discover good solutions rather than answers, solutions that were theirs, not the tutor's. Unfortunately, this process, which has generally served native-speaking writers well (Harris, Leahy) and is justifiably a source of pride for those who can make it work, was often ineffective for our second-language writers, especially those confronting college-level writing in English for the first time.

Perhaps the major reason for this failure is the difference in what the two groups of writers bring to the writing center conference. Most native-speaking writers, for better or for worse, have come to us with comparatively broad and predictable experiences of writing and writing instruction in English. When they have problems with some concept or technique, it is therefore relatively easy for writing center faculty to intuit the source of their difficulty and adjust our questioning to help them discover new, more workable principles. A writer, for example, who is trying to force two points (or four points) into three paragraphs is likely to have been drilled in the five-paragraph essay format and can be guided fairly easily to discover that not all ideas break down into three parts. ESL writers, however, seldom come to the writing center conference with any substantial background in writing and writing instruction in English. Attempts, therefore, to play off such experience in devising collaborative strategies are likely to fail.

Furthermore, ESL writers typically come to the writing center conference with first-language rhetorics different from the rhetoric of academic English with which they are struggling (Grabe and Kaplan; Leki). Since what these writers already know about writing is based in those first-language rhetorics, it is likely that attempts to use common collaborative strategies will backfire and lead them away from, not toward, the solutions they seek. Consider, for example, the common and fairly simple problem of helping a writer understand that a conclusion should contain no new, unsupported ideas. While it is fairly easy to impress a native-speaking writer with the logic of this rule (because the term *conclusion* itself implies it), the rule is not at all logical to writers from cultures where effective conclusions do, in fact, include new ideas. In this, as in other conferencing situations, those attempting to assist second-language writers may be hampered not only by the writers' limited backgrounds in the rhetoric of written English but also by their learned patterns as educated writers of their own languages. As another example, bringing ESL writers to see the logic of placing important material at the beginnings of English paragraphs may, at times, involve overriding their long-time cultural assumptions that such material should appear at the end. Because collaborative techniques depend so heavily on shared basic assumptions or patterns, conferences that attempt merely to take the techniques we use with native-speaking writers and apply them to ESL writers may fail to assist the writers we intend to help.

The sense of audience that ESL writers bring to the writing center has also affected the success of our typical conferencing strategy. Experienced writing center faculty can lead native-speaking writers to a fuller awareness of certain writing principles through questions about their audience—what the members of their audience already know about a subject, what purpose a reader might have for reading their piece of writing, what kind of people make up their audience and what qualities will impress that group. Using this Socratic technique, in fact, helps us avoid the didactic role of identifying correct and incorrect approaches. However, second-language writers, already handicapped by an unfamiliar rhetoric, are likely to be writing to an unfamiliar audience as well. Part of what they need from us is knowledge of what that unknown audience will expect, need, and find convincing. Thus, ESL writers are asking us to become audiences for their work in a broader way than native speakers are; they view us as cultural informants about American academic expectations.

Predictably, as a result of these differences in the educational, rhetorical, and cultural contexts of ESL writers, our faculty found themselves increasingly in the role of informant rather than collaborator. We were becoming more direct, more didactic in our approach, teaching writing to ESL writers essentially as an academic subject.

Understanding the Need for Intervention

In this shifted role lay the crux of the difficulty we increasingly experienced with ESL conferencing. Because our whole writing center philosophy—our Socratic, nondirective approach—was (and is) geared away from the notion that we are teachers of an academic subject, it was not easy for us to see ourselves as cultural/rhetorical informants with valuable information to impart. One unfortunate result of this situation was that writing center faculty tended to define conferences where ESL writers got what they needed from us (i.e., direct help) as failures rather than successes.

This problem occurred in ESL conferences involving all aspects of writing. Writing center instructors found themselves, for example, telling writers what their audiences would expect rather than asking the writers to decide, answering questions about the sufficiency of the evidence provided in a particular context rather than leaving that decision to the writer, or showing writers how to say something rather than asking them what they wanted to say. When such exchanges occurred, we found it difficult to view them from the standpoint of the ESL writer for whom the conference might have been a success; rather, we measured them against our nondirective philosophy which we appeared to have betrayed.

The distance between the needs of the ESL writer and the assumptions of the system has perhaps been most apparent in conferences where ESL writers have come to us for help with editing and proofing. Like many writing centers, the University of Wyoming Writing Center handles the perennial problem of students wanting drafts edited with a policy statement: We will teach writers editing and proofing strategies but will not edit or proof for them. This distinction serves us reasonably well when dealing with native-speaking writers. It is less successful, however, in setting workable parameters for ESL conferences, partly because our ESL conferees have difficulty understanding the line it draws, but mostly because the techniques we use to teach editing/proofing strategies to native-speaking writers seldom work for ESL writers. These techniques, which largely involve reading aloud and learning to use the ear to edit, presume that the writer hears the language correctly and is more familiar and comfortable with the oral than the written word. Native-speaking writers reading aloud can typically locate problem passages, which we can then discuss with them, suggesting principles upon which they can base editing decisions. In this scenario, we hope writers learn to raise and answer their own questions.

Neither reading aloud nor editing by ear appears to work for the majority of ESL writers we see, however. Few beginning second-language writers "hear" the language "correctly," and many are more familiar with written than with spoken English. Since they have no inner editor prompting them to stop and raise questions, we are likely to adjust our technique to their needs and discover we are locating errors for ESL writers in a way that looks very much like editing. When we find ourselves backed into this situation, we immediately begin to raise questions about our appropriation of writers' texts, an anathema in writing center methodology not only for practical reasons inherent in working with classroom assignments but also because our aim is to demystify writing for conferees and increase their self-reliance and self-confidence. While the intervention that ESL writers appear to require of us in working with editing problems does not differ greatly from the intervention involved when we assist those same writers with rhetorical structure and audience, it strikes us more forcibly because it is familiar and easy to perceive. In fact, it looks very much like the "bad" kind of help native speakers sometimes want when they bring papers in to be "corrected."

The mixed feelings that the ESL editing issue engendered were not a new problem for the writing center. Throughout our history, we had faced and handled requests for assistance in editing ESL texts, responding to them more or less on a case-by-case basis, with varying levels of confidence in our decisions. Almost every semester, for example, the demand for editorial assistance with ESL theses and dissertations reaches the point at which writing center faculty begin to complain in frustration about ESL writers expecting them to correct and rewrite texts. Each year, the staff has vowed to establish a clearer policy that will prevent abuses of the system, discussed the subject vigorously, realized that doing so would limit the open-door policy we value so much, and consequently let the subject slide.

The primary difference between our past ESL conferencing experiences and our experiences of the last two years was our awareness of an emerging pattern in ESL conferencing that called into question some of our fundamental assumptions about what we do. Increased numbers of second-language conferences, as well as conferences involving a larger variety of writing tasks, highlighted difficulties in applying our traditional conferencing strategies to all aspects of second-language writing, not just editing. What had once appeared scattered instances of ineffectiveness in our typical approach became symptomatic of a broader inability to meet the needs of ESL writers with the same basic methods we use to assist native speakers. This realization led us to question whether our past reluctance to confront directly the issues involved in ESL conferencing was really the benign neglect we had assumed it to be or whether we were unintentionally undermining the principles we meant to protect and distancing ourselves from the needs of a large group of writers.

Adapting Conferencing Strategies to Assist ESL Writers

Once genuinely convinced that traditional collaborative strategies often do not work with ESL writers, our faculty realized that the key to more effective ESL conferencing was an attitude adjustment on our part. We had to accept that ESL writers bring different contexts to conferences than native speakers do, that they are, therefore, likely to need different kinds of assistance from us, and that successful assistance to ESL writers may involve more intervention in their writing processes than we consider appropriate with native-speaking writers.

For those of us whose experience has demonstrated the virtues of nondirective conferencing techniques, simple acceptance of the need to adopt more directive strategies was not always an easy first step. Part of the difficulty in taking this step stemmed from the fact that the differences between native-speaking and second-language writers are sometimes masked by a deceiving familiarity in what they say and do. When native-speaking writers come into the writing center expecting us to tell them what is *the answer* to a problem or the *right* way to express an idea, we may see them—often quite rightly—as either "timid" writers who need their self-confidence boosted, teacher-dependent writers who want an authority to appropriate their writing, or "lazy" writers who want someone else to do their work. In any of these cases, we see our job as getting the writer to assume responsibility for the writing. ESL writers who come to us expecting answers to questions about where their thesis statements should appear, how many developmental paragraphs they must have, how much and what kind of support a point requires, or how an idea should be phrased too often appear to fall into one of these categories: they appear to be insecure, to be abdicating responsibility for their texts for one of the above reasons.

Although the questions that ESL writers ask us are deceivingly similar to the questions native speakers sometimes raise, the contexts of the questions make them substantially different. What we discovered is that failure to recognize the essential difference in these seemingly similar questions severely undercuts our ability to assist second-language writers in acquiring the academic writing skills they need. If we assumed such writers were shy or dependent writers who merely needed encouragement to take charge of their texts, and if we adopted our usual collaborative approach to bring about that recognition of ownership, we were unlikely to achieve our accustomed results because we were applying an attitude solution to an information problem. If we assumed the worst—that the writers were lazy and were trying to get us to take over the writing—we might be travelling even further toward the wrong solution, based on the wrong evidence. We were, in fact, unlikely to provide useful help to ESL writers until we saw the questions they raised about basic form and usage not as evasions of responsibility but as the real questions of writers struggling with an unfamiliar culture, audience, and rhetoric.

To extend the benefits of conferencing and collaborative learning to ESL writers, writing center faculty must understand what these writers need from us and how their needs differ from those of native-speaking writers. The principal difference in the two conferencing situations appears to be the increased emphasis on our role as informant (rather than collaborator) in the second-language conference. Because we know little about ESL writers' rhetorics, backgrounds, and cultures, and because they know little about their current academic discourse community and the rhetoric of academic English, we can assist them only by becoming more direct in our approach, by teaching them writing as an academic subject. Doing so may, in fact, involve teaching them directly what their writing should look like by supplying them with formats for presenting written responses to various academic assignments and informing them of what their audiences will expect in terms of presentation, evidence, shape, etc.

Conclusion

Although collaborative learning is not a familiar process to most of the international students we see in the writing center, and some of the Socratic techniques we have developed as a result of this theory do not serve the ESL population particularly well, collaborative writing and conference teaching do work for these writers in some important ways. As with native-speaking writers, the process of verbalizing an idea often helps ESL writers discover a direction, and the act of sketching a structure (even with the help of a faculty member) clarifies the principles of that construct in a way merely reading about it cannot. ESL writers who describe their conferencing experiences mention a new awareness of audience, a clarification of the principles of organization, and the discovery of new vocabulary and sentence structures as benefits. In fact, just by acquiring a vocabulary to discuss their writing in English, second-language writers make a first step toward understanding and self-sufficiency.

But these benefits of collaboration accrue to ESL writers through *successful* writing center conferences. We can assist ESL writers to become more capable writers of English only if we understand what they bring to the writing center conference and allow that perspective to determine our conferencing strategies. Structuring successful ESL conferences probably requires that we reexamine our approach as outsiders might, making a real attempt to discard the rhetoric and patterns of thought that are so familiar to us as to seem inevitable. We might, for example, better assist our second-language writers by analyzing academic assignments from an outside perspective to see exactly what *is* expected in American academic prose, gathering information about audience expectations that recognize our culturally based assumptions, and learning to ask questions in conferences that will allow ESL writers to understand more about idea generation and presentation of evidence. Conferences based on this information and approach might appear different, on the surface, from conferences we conduct with native-speaking writers, but they bring us closer to accomplishing our writing center's goal of providing meaningful help to all campus writers with all kinds of writing questions.

When writing center faculty, with the best of intentions, apply collaborative techniques devised for native-speaking writers to ESL writers, the possibility of cultural miscommunication and failed conferences is inherent in the methodology itself. Since its inception, our writing center has struggled in concern and frustration over a frequent inability to make ESL conferences both successful for the participants and consistent with our conferencing philosophy. In retrospect, it appears that much of this struggle basically involved attempts to determine which of the conference participants was responsible for conferences that failed to meet one or both of these criteria. Sometimes we concluded that the writer was at fault for refusing to accept responsibility for the text and thereby undermining the collaborative process. More frequently, we blamed ourselves for failing to apply our conferencing principles and techniques appropriately or allowing ourselves to be drawn into directive conferencing by an unusually clever or forceful writer. Our experience of the past two years has convinced us that we will increase the effectiveness of ESL conferencing only when we understand, accept, and respond to the differences between the needs of ESL and native-speaking writers. Attempts to reform or reshape the participants in the conference are unlikely to prove effectual; we must reexamine and revise the method itself.

Note

[1]Our ESL population (currently 465 students) is almost exclusively international students who have studied English in their own countries before coming to the United States. The largest group of students come from China, India, Malaysia, Norway, and Taiwan; they have achieved a minimum TOEFL score of 525 and have been admitted to the university.

Works Cited

Grabe, William, and Robert B. Kaplan. "Writing in a Second Language: Contrastive Rhetoric." *Richness in Writing: Empowering ESL Students.* Ed. Donna Johnson and Duane Roen. New York: Longman, 1989.

Harris, Muriel. "What's Up and What's In: Trends and Traditions in Writing Centers." *The Writing Center Journal* 11 (1990): 15-25.

Leahy, Richard. "What the College Writing Center Is—and Isn't." *College Teaching* 38 (1990): 43-48.

Leki, Ilona. "Twenty-five Years of Contrastive Rhetoric: Text Analysis and Writing Pedagogies." *TESOL Quarterly* 25 (1991): 123-43.

"Thirty-something" Students: Concerning Transitions in the Writing Center

Cynthia Haynes-Burton
THE UNIVERSITY OF TEXAS AT DALLAS

As companies "downsize" and various industries lay off workers, many adults are returning to school to pursue a second career. To help them face their new challenges, tutors must recognize that "thirty-something" students have needs that differ from those of traditional students. Nontraditional students often suffer anxiety when confronted by a loss of the stability and identity their previous careers gave them. Most will likely balance multiple family and work roles in addition to assuming their new roles as students. They may also be reluctant to ask for help with their writing, and, when they do, they may tend to focus on basic problems with grammar and mechanics rather than on overall structure or support for their ideas. Writing centers are well suited to help nontraditional students make the transition back to school, Cynthia Haynes-Burton says. When such students "establish a solid relationship with the writing center," they can regain a sense of security they have lost. Tutors can help reduce the anxieties of nontraditional students by "showing them how to channel the confidence they possess in other areas of their life and apply it to writing problems." Her essay demonstrates the sensitivity to different circumstances and life experiences that a successful collaborative relationship between tutor and nontraditional student requires. This essay originally appeared in Writing Lab Newsletter *in 1990.*

IT WOULD NOT BE EXAGGERATING TO SAY that there has been an enormous growth in the *industry* of composition instruction; yet, until recently, we often defined our field in terms of static theories and practical pedagogies rather than across the fertile chaos that this industry has spawned. Ironically, the effects of dynamism and flux in composition theory have produced a backlash of centrism, or the nostalgia for a stable "center." In contrast, the realities of writing instruction, and writing centers in particular, cry out for affirmation of change, of drifting in and out of stable centers. In their collection of essays, editors Ray Wallace and Jeanne Simpson note the common thread that "writing centers are dynamic, not static, that change and adjustment to new problems come with the territory" (xiii). I am interested in isolating this notion of change in terms of the effect on the writing center of one particular subculture within the composition field, the growing population of older college students—people who are living models for the process of change.

One of the most extreme effects of this process of change is the feeling of displacement, whether physical or conceptual. For example, in the past twenty years, due to the advent of corporate mergers, lay-offs, hiring freezes, staff contractions and realignments, consolidations, and attrition, we have seen a rapid growth in career transitions. When these forced displacements occur, many people return to college, or choose to begin their post-secondary education for the first time. As these individuals enter college, the demographics of our student populations change drastically. While this growing diversity in age creates the need for new strategies in the classroom, it also represents an immediate challenge for the writing center.

An important first step in addressing the needs of older students in the writing center would be to recruit tutors from all age groups. Not only is it important to hire or appoint tutors with diverse disciplinary backgrounds and good writing skills, it is equally important to mirror the ethnic, gender, and age differences of the general student population of any institution. There are, however, other models for consideration. For example, Susan Kleimann and G. Douglas Meyers created a unique program in their writing center in which senior citizens volunteered to work as writing tutors. According to Kleimann and Meyers, these tutors bring their experience in the non-academic world to bear on the students' writing. Many of them were retired professionals such as former librarians, professors, engineers, etc. Their practical experience introduced a level of maturity and authenticity that traditional-aged "peer tutors" often do not yet possess. If we look at the reverse of this situation, we must also ask how traditional-aged peer tutors and older student writers work together. The answer lies in redefining the "peer" relationship.

The concept of peer tutoring has recently come under scrutiny, most notably in John Trimbur's essay, "Peer Tutoring: A Contradiction in Terms?" Trimbur's concerns center on the tutor training process which he claims can often send contradictory signals to tutors who are being trained as "little teachers" while also being encouraged to identify themselves as "peers" of other student writers. Trimbur argues that "if peer tutoring programs are efforts by educators to tap the identification of student with student as a potentially powerful source of learning, peer tutoring can also lead to the further identification of peer tutors with the system that has rewarded them, underscoring the tutors' personal stake in the hierarchical values of higher education" (24). Trimbur suggests that the conflict between the "apprentice" model and the "co-learner" model of tutor training reproduces the contradictory experience of "peer" and "tutor" that students "experience at a gut level" (26). His solution is a "sequence of tutor training that treats tutors differently depending on their tutoring experience—in short, that treats tutors developmentally" (26).

I agree with Trimbur in principle, that "peer tutoring" is a contradiction in terms; but, the contradiction goes deeper than this when tutors face older student writers. Rather than introduce new terminology to describe the "peer tutor," I suggest that we need to ask ourselves whether, given these dynamics, peer tutoring as a concept is capable of properly characterizing what it is that goes on in the writing center; and, more importantly, we need to redefine the relationship between tutor and writer across different bases. The issue of tutor training, like any pedagogical contact, immediately introduces theoretical disputes, socialization concerns, and pragmatic challenges. Writing center practitioners have struggled with these issues in great detail. I am suggesting that we also need to define the role of the writing center tutor in terms of transitional concerns.

In his recent book, *Transitions*, William Bridges reminds us that "every transition begins with an ending" (11). When people go back to school there is an anxiety associated with "starting over" so late in life. Bridges argues that this is part of a mentality that says the earlier part of our life was a mistake or that now it is time to catch up to everyone else. In addition, Bridges claims that it is harder to teach older adults "process" because the world is so mechanistic, so product-oriented. We see ourselves as something not-yet-finished. In the writing center this is often why older students perceive their writing errors as "malfunctions." Against this, Bridges encourages us to view transitions as a time of readjustment and renewed commitment, rather than as "the confusing nowhere of in-betweenness" (5). He sees life as "unfolding," as a series of alternating periods of stability and change. According to Bridges, transitions in career signal a change from being motivated by the chance to demonstrate competence to being motivated by the chance to find meaning.

One manifestation of this difference in motivation is the difficulty that older students experience when faced with the "freedom" to choose their own topic for writing assignments. The problem is that in addition to its positive effects, *freedom is also something we fear.* Yet, in the writing center, freedom is often a banner under which we march to justify and tout our non-directive tutoring philosophies. We must be aware that the effect of unexpected freedom is sometimes the loss of structure, whether it is the structure of a job or a piece of writing. The implication of this for tutor training is to maintain a delicate balance between freedom and structure for both tutors and writers. The experiences of older students teach us that the involuntary loss of structure is a lesson we all need to heed in order to qualify our writing center theories and pedagogies.

Some of my older students tell me that when they enter the writing center, they do so with additional motives and different assumptions about what writing and tutoring can accomplish. Often returning students come to the writing center asking advice about which freshman writing courses to take to help them "brush up" on their grammar. They explain that it has been ten, fifteen, or twenty years since their last English course, and they are no longer confident of their grammar and style skills. In some cases, they appear in a panic and highly insecure about their chances for a successful re-entry into college. It is not difficult to imagine visions of red ink in their memories of freshman composition or diagramming sentences in a code they no longer remember. I do not discourage these students from taking such courses now. I do, however, encourage them to consider their options. For example, I explain that most freshman composition programs actually integrate reading, writing, and critical thinking skills. They will be reading essays in order to respond with an expository or argumentative essay of their own. I explain how their writing will be evaluated in terms of organization, support for their ideas, and clear and cohesive prose rather than strictly on the basis of grammar and style. I suggest alternative courses that focus on grammar and style, but these often do not count toward their degree. The best alternative, and the one they choose most often, is to establish a solid relationship with the writing center. I assign a specific tutor to work with them on a regular basis. Sometimes the student and tutor work together on specific writing projects, sometimes the tutor creates an assignment for them, and sometimes they just talk. The result is that students gain the confidence in writing that matches the confidence they possess in other areas, like jobs or families.

In some ways these students are no different from traditional-aged students. That is, they face identical assignments and harbor similar anxieties about writing and grades that a large dose of confidence will often help to resolve. On the other hand, they face these anxieties with a different set of experiences and expectations. For example, many of them are more organized in their approach to assignments, yet they are less confident of their ability to convey their thoughts. In these instances, it is simply a matter of showing them how to channel the confidence they possess in other areas of their life and apply it to writing problems.

One returning student, I'll call him Steve, came to the writing center because he was having trouble understanding his teacher's assignment to write an interpretive paper on a poem the class was studying. Steve had received a "C" on his paper. His teacher claimed he had not supported his conclusions. Steve did not understand his instructor's expectations, and he simply could not see what he was doing wrong. Prior to coming to the writing center, he had made an appointment elsewhere to test for [a] learning disability, thinking that he had some dysfunction. Steve had convinced himself that he was impaired because he did not understand his assignment. In addition, Steve seemed embarrassed to ask for help; yet, Steve's reluctance to seek help is typical of adult learners who have shifted from dependency to independency. Unlike most traditional-aged students, older students are no longer dependent upon their parents for support and encouragement. In fact, many of these students are working parents who balance multiple roles in their family and at work. I encouraged Steve often to keep this in mind when his lack of confidence in writing seemed overwhelming.

After Steve and I worked together for an entire semester we both learned some valuable lessons about writing and learning. I learned that older students have unique needs and have a great deal of experience to bring to their writing and to the tutoring session itself. Each time Steve came in the door, I threw caution to the wind and looked for ways to encourage the elements of transition and change I witnessed in his writing, as well as the confidence I could see gradually emerging. Steve did not improve his grade on the "C" paper, but he worked hard on subsequent papers and eventually improved to his own satisfaction. The following semester Steve became president of *Encore*, our university organization for older and returning non traditional students over the age of twenty-one.

Since my first session with Steve, I have worked with many older student writers, hired several older "writing assistants," and set up an office for *Encore* in the writing center, and I am working on a proposal for a major grant to develop an organized writing center program to meet the needs of older nontraditional students. With the defense spending cut back, many military support personnel will soon be displaced. These events are also part of a general trend in local business to "downsize" companies through staff "realignments." In light of these alarming trends in job elimination in the United States, all American universities and community colleges face new challenges as these displaced individuals re-enter the education process. I believe writing centers can move to the front line of responding to the needs of older students. Christina Murphy puts it best: "if writing centers are to become true 'centers' of outreach amongst disciplines, they must also become true centers of outreach for communities and whole regions" (284).

Works Cited

Bridges, William. *Transitions: Making Sense of Life's Changes*. Reading: Addison-Wesley, 1980.

Kleimann, Susan, and G. Douglas Meyers. "Senior Citizens and Junior Writers: A Center for Exchange." *Writing Center Journal*. 2.1 (1982): 57–60.

Murphy, Christina. "Writing Centers in Context: Responding to Current Educational Theory." *The Writing Center: New Directions*. Ed. Ray Wallace and Jeanne Simpson. New York: Garland, 1991. 276–88.

Trimbur, John. "Peer Tutoring: A Contradiction in Terms?" *Writing Center Journal* 7.2 (1987): 21–28.

Wallace, Ray, and Jeanne Simpson, eds. *The Writing Center: New Directions*. New York: Garland, 1991.

Multi-sensory Tutoring for Multi-sensory Learners

*Shoshana Beth Konstant*_____

Shoshana Beth Konstant offers strategies for tutors to help students with learning disabilities, whom she describes as multi-sensory learners. "Most learning disabled college students can learn most things when presented with information in an appropriate manner," Konstant claims. Tutors should "determine how a student learns best and teach to that," she urges. Recognizing "the student's strongest perceptual channel" enables the tutor to tailor advice to reinforce the student's preferred ways of learning. Tutors will benefit from knowing the range of approaches Konstant suggests for assisting visual, auditory, and kinesthetic learners. Her essay, which first appeared in 1992 in Writing Lab Newsletter, *provides important background information on learning disabilities and the information-processing styles of multi-sensory learners. Konstant points out that tutors are not diagnosticians of learning disabilities—that role belongs to neurologists and other trained professionals. Instead, tutors can be important allies by helping to eliminate stereotypical thinking about students who are able and motivated learners but who process information differently from the majority of their fellow students.*

THE FIELD OF LEARNING DISABILITIES SEEMS FRAUGHT with conflict; some experts say that learning disabilities are strictly a result of neurological problems, while others will swear that at least some are developmental in nature. Armed camps vehemently defend their positions about whether to teach to the student's strengths or weaknesses. Whether or not these battles will ever by won by one side or the other is anyone's guess (though technological advances in the ability to study brain functioning do seem to be revealing more and more minute damage that was previously undetectable—score one for the neurologists). But I am not a neurologist, nor am I a developmental theorist. I am a tutor, and I'm not sure I care who's right or who wins. The causes of learning disabilities are important to know in order to remediate the problem (if you are of the camp who believes that they are a problem), but whether or not to remediate is another whole argument in itself, and remediation isn't my job, anyway.

Defining a learning disability is as difficult and controversial as everything else about the field. For purposes of our discussion here, it is a perceptual or processing problem, possibly neurologically based, which results in the person acting on perceptions different from those of most people. More simply put, learning disabled (LD) people might read "reason" as "raisin" not because they don't know the word, but merely because they don't see the difference—similar to the way some people can't perceive the difference between red and green. The characteristic of LD students that is easiest to forget and most important to remember is that they possess an average IQ.

One way of dealing with learning disabilities that has proven helpful to educators is to determine how a student learns best and to teach to that. Assuming that learning involves taking in and processing information, tutors who employ this method try to present information through the student's strongest perceptual channel (i.e., way of taking in information; "channel" is just jargon that makes you sound like you know what you're talking about).

The primary channels are visual, auditory, and kinesthetic. Visual learners can best process and remember information that they see, be it in the form of charts, diagrams, pictures, or printed text. Auditory learners do best with verbal explanations or discussions. Kinesthetic learners need to move or do things; this type of learning, being the most unfamiliar to and unused by most of us, is the most difficult to explain.

We all have our own preferred ways of learning, and these often vary with the task. For example, I can never do my ballet routines correctly unless I do them while the teacher demonstrates, but I can sometimes figure out the dynamics of an ecosystem just by staring at it long enough. The former is an example of kinesthetic learning, while the latter is visual. I am primarily a visual learner: I prefer to read things for myself or read along when someone reads to me, as I have trouble understanding what other people read to me.

Many learning disabled students know how they learn best and will tell you at the beginning of the tutoring session if you ask. It is worth taking the time to find out, particularly with students whom you work with repeatedly. Why spend twenty minutes verbally explaining something to a visual learner? Why not teach to the student's strengths? The technical term for this approach, by the way, is Aptitude-Treatment Interaction (ATI), and one of the chief criticisms of it is that it becomes too formulaic: Learning style A + Teaching style A = Success. This trait is also, of course, its most attractive feature for some—the same people, I suspect, who want a rule for every possible use of a comma.

But punctuation is most often intuitive, and so is tutoring. The best tutoring sometimes occurs when all theory goes out the window. The single most important piece of advice I can give as someone experienced in tutoring LD students is do whatever works. Do anything to get the message across. I have ranted, raved, and stood on desks. Tutoring LD students is a chance to exercise one's creativity. Standard explanations or tutoring techniques may prove to be completely worthless for some students; in fact, what worked wonders for one learning disabled student may leave the next nonplussed, even confused. Don't despair. Try something else. Have patience; the student is infinitely more frustrated than you are. Try every possible way you can think of to get your message across and if they all fail, then try something else.

Try ways of reaching the student through more than one channel at a time. Use combinations of visual, auditory, and kinesthetic techniques—the multisensory approach. Say it and draw it; read text aloud; use color to illustrate things. For example, when I wanted to show a student how often he had used simple sentences, we underlined simple sentences in red, complex in blue, and compound in green. Then we taped the paper to the wall, stood ten feet away, and saw that the majority of the paper was red. Nothing I could ever have said to this man would have made as strong an impression as this did.

Knowing a student's learning strengths is useful, not in order to apply specific techniques but as general background information. Being aware, for instance, that someone is a visual learner might remind you to draw diagrams of organizational patterns when discussing them or to highlight in color all topic sentences; however, it doesn't mean that you must do all these things every time. The following lists are meant to be suggestions, not requirements. Do what works with each individual. Most learning disabled college students can learn most things when presented with information in an appropriate manner.

Techniques for Tutoring Learning Disabled Students

I. Visual techniques

- Present information visually whenever possible. Use charts, diagrams, pictures, graphs, or concrete visual examples.
- Work from written material when possible, pointing to the information being discussed.
- Use a chalkboard to illustrate points.
- When possible, use colors (chalk or pens) to differentiate material: to highlight topic sentences, to put in punctuation, to distinguish between fact and inference, etc.
- Use gestures when explaining a point. Be animated—point, circle the information, draw a picture, act it out—involve yourself in the information.
- Use concrete visual images when possible.
- Make sure the student leaves the session with a visual representation, such as notes and/or diagrams, of what has been discussed verbally.

II. Auditory techniques

- Use auditory reinforcement of visually presented material. Read notes and papers aloud while pointing to the material.
- Verbally discuss all major points for reinforcement.
- Have the student read aloud.
- Encourage the student to use a tape recorder for tutoring sessions and classes so material can be reviewed at home.
- Have the student study with a tape recorder. Information should be read aloud and played back several times.

- Encourage the student to use a tape recorder to do written assignments, dictating ideas or entire sentences which can be transcribed later.

III. Kinesthetic techniques

- Allow the student to do the writing, copying, underlining, highlighting, moving.
- Make rearranging of items a physical activity for the student. Instead of drawing arrows to indicate where a sentence or paragraph should be moved to, put phrases, clauses, ideas, sentences, or paragraphs on separate pieces of paper or cards which the student can physically rearrange.
- Act things out and/or have the student act them out.
- Have the student copy (write over) information to be remembered.
- Use gestures when speaking and point to the material being discussed or read. Have students point as they read or discuss as well.
- If students have problems remembering terms used in tutoring discussion, develop with students a system of gestures they can use instead.

IV. Multi-sensory techniques

- Present information in as many ways as possible: say it and write it, draw it and discuss it, discuss it and act it out.
- Develop color, abbreviation, sound, or gesture systems for concepts which the student understands but can't remember names for.
- Combine techniques whenever and to whatever extent possible. For example, have the student read something aloud while pointing to or highlighting it; thus, the student is getting visual, auditory, and kinesthetic input.
- Be animated; involve the student in the session and encourage active participation.
- Be creative. Try to think of new ways to convey what you are expressing. Don't repeat the same explanation two or three or seven times; the student is no more likely to understand it the seventh time than the first. Find ways of communicating through the student's strongest perceptual channels.

PART

III

Resources for Further Inquiry

The burgeoning interest in writing centers over the past several decades has created a wealth of informative resources for tutors, ranging from scholarly journals to videotapes of the collaborative process. In addition to print and video sources, tutors also can find support for their work in regional and national organizations and on electronic networks.

Because writing center work has always respected the value of individual narratives and case studies, scholarship in the field often includes examples drawn from tutors' actual practice. This approach helps make writing center scholarship accessible to novice tutors, who will appreciate the conversational style of the journals and will find much to identify with in the case studies and narrative examples they include.

NATIONAL WRITING CENTERS ASSOCIATION

The primary professional group for writing center personnel is the National Writing Centers Association (NWCA). The NWCA promotes writing center causes and provides educational materials and support services related to writing center practice. Among its many services, the NWCA publishes a national directory of high school, community college, and college and university writing centers; sponsors a national conference and lends support to nine regional organizations and conferences; gives awards for outstanding scholarship on writing centers; offers information and assistance from its committees that research and investigate issues such as peer tutoring, writing centers and writing across the curriculum, and writing centers and graduate education; and provides a free "starter kit" for setting up a writing center. Information on NWCA and its nine regional affiliates is available from Alan Jackson, Executive Secretary, NWCA, Dekalb College, 2101 Womack Road, Dunwoody, Georgia 30338, (404) 551-3207.

JOURNALS

Writing center work has three journals devoted exclusively to its concerns: *The Writing Lab Newsletter*, edited by Muriel Harris of Purdue University; *The Writing Center Journal*, edited by Dave Healey of the University of Minnesota; and *Focuses: A Journal Linking Composition Programs and Writing-Center Practice*, edited

113

by William C. Wolff of Appalachian State University and sponsored by the Southeastern Writing Centers Association. *The Writing Lab Newsletter* and *The Writing Center Journal* are sponsored by the National Writing Centers Association.

The Writing Lab Newsletter provides news on conferences and meetings as well as columns, letters, and scholarly articles on writing center practice. It regularly publishes a column on peer tutoring as well as articles by peer tutors. The newsletter is respected for its accessible style and its capacity to convey the voices of writing center personnel at work. By contrast, *The Writing Center Journal* and *Focuses* publish more theoretical and scholarly articles. Both journals offer annual annotated bibliographies of scholarship on writing centers.

Two additional journals that often include articles on writing centers and tutoring are *Composition Studies* and *Dialogue: A Journal for Writing Specialists*. *English Journal, Research in the Teaching of English, Journal of Basic Writing*, and *Teaching English in the Two-Year College* also publish occasional articles on writing centers and related topics.

BOOKS

Books on writing centers, like the scholarly articles, tend to focus to varying degrees on practice, administration, or theory. Among those that emphasize practice, the following books provide rationales, strategies, and techniques for conducting tutorials, as well as informative scenarios of actual tutoring sessions:

Harris, Muriel. *Teaching One-to-One: The Writing Conference*. Urbana: NCTE, 1986.
Maxwell, Martha, ed. *When Tutor Meets Student*. Ann Arbor: U of Michigan P, 1994.
Meyer, Emily, and Louise Z. Smith. *The Practical Tutor*. New York: Oxford UP, 1987.

In addition, *The Bedford Guide for Writing Tutors* by Leigh Ryan (Boston: Bedford, 1994) focuses on the same concerns but presents its information in a condensed fashion, as a kind of "how-to" manual for beginning tutors.

The following books discuss the administration of writing centers in terms of issues such as start-up, staffing, developing peer tutor programs, and addressing the needs of special student populations:

Clark, Irene Lurkis. *Writing in the Center: Teaching in a Writing Center*. Dubuque: Kendall/Hunt, 1985.
Olson, Gary A., ed. *Writing Centers: Theory and Administration*. Urbana: NCTE, 1984.
Steward, Joyce, and Mary Croft. *The Writing Laboratory: Organization, Methods, and Management*. Glenview: Scott, Foresman, 1982.

Olson's statement that "tutorial writing services have always been diverse in their pedagogies, philosophies, and physical makeups" (vii) indicates the lines of inquiry these books pursue. In addition, *Writing Centers in Context: Twelve Case Studies*, edited by Joyce A. Kinkead and Jeanette G. Harris (Urbana: NCTE, 1993) presents profiles of "twelve particular programs—detailed descriptions of how each came into being and how it functions" (xv). Kinkead and Harris examine writing centers in "small private liberal arts colleges and large state universities; medium-sized land grant colleges as well as two-year colleges and four-year institutions; schools located in urban and in rural areas and on the east and west coast and in between" (xvi). Their book demonstrates that "diverse perspectives define writing centers much more accurately than could any single definition of an abstract, model center" (xvii).

Two collections of essays by noted professionals focus on writing center theory:

Mullin, Joan, and Ray Wallace, eds. *Intersections: Theory-Practice in the Writing Center*. Urbana: NCTE, 1994.
Wallace, Ray, and Jeanne Simpson, eds. *The Writing Center: New Directions*. New York: Garland, 1991.

Wallace and Simpson state that their collection presents "a much-needed investigation into how writing centers identify new roles, new constituencies, and new methodologies across our college and university curricula" (ix). Current trends, writing center outreach, satellite writing centers, the role of writing centers in student retention, the relationship of writing centers to classroom instruction, and writing centers and educational theory are among the topics considered. *Intersections* discusses writing center theory and practice in relation to cultural studies and rhetorical theory and examines such philosophical perspectives as social constructionism, social-epistemic rhetoric, and feminist theory. Both books are useful to tutors as an introduction to the major theories and professional issues in the field.

VIDEOTAPES

Two videotapes on tutoring and collaborative learning are *Beginning Writing Groups* and *Student Writing Groups: Demonstrating the Process*. Both videotapes show "real-time demonstrations of a writing group at work." Students read essays aloud and receive feedback from their peers. Afterwards, group members discuss the benefits of writing groups and collaborative learning. The purpose of the videotapes is "to model structure and process" and to show how the group process can be adapted "to a variety of writing tasks and requirements." Each videotape is around 30 minutes long and is helpful in modeling collaborative writing, problem solving, and training exercises for beginning tutors. An accompanying booklet provides an annotated bibliography of articles on writing groups and a "trouble-shooting" guide for resolving problems that can arise in group work. The videotapes are available from Wordshop Productions, 3832 N. 7th St., Tacoma, Washington 98406, (206) 759-6953.

ELECTRONIC NETWORK

WCenter is the leading electronic network for online discussions of writing center work. WCenter lets writing center personnel share information, seek answers to inquiries, pose questions for further investigation, and establish a sense of community. Anyone with access to Bitnet or Internet can subscribe to WCenter by sending an E-mail message to LISTPROC@UNICORN. ACS.TTU.EDU Leave the subject line blank. On the first line, type *Subscribe WCenter <your first name> <your last name>* Then complete your computer system's procedures for sending electronic mail messages.

WCenter provides an important way for writing center personnel to share the immediacy of their work and concerns. It is one confirming example of Jeanne Simpson's view that "the writing center movement has expanded because writing center people have learned to communicate—to form a network, to transmit information, and to exchange assistance" ("What Lies Ahead for Writing Centers: Position Statement on Professional Concerns," *The Writing Center Journal* 5.2 and 6.1 [1985]: 35-39).

GRAMMAR HOTLINE DIRECTORY

A *Grammar Hotline Directory*, updated each January, is available from Tidewater Community College. The directory lists telephone services in the United States and Canada that provide free answers to short questions about writing and grammar. Single copies are free; multiple copies cost $1.00 each. Send a self-addressed, stamped envelope to *Grammar Hotline Directory*, Tidewater Community College Writing Center, 1700 College Crescent, Virginia Beach, Virginia 23456. For further information, contact Donna Reiss, Writing Center/Grammar Hotline Director, at (804) 427-7170.